Footsteps Back to Primal

by Quinn Arbogast

DORRANCE
PUBLISHING CO
EST. 1920
PITTSBURGH, PENNSYLVANIA 15238

Dorrance Publishing Co
585 Alpha Drive
Suite 103
Pittsburgh, PA 15238
Visit our website at *www.dorrancebookstore.com*

ISBN: 979-8-8860-4091-3
eISBN: 979-8-8860-4990-9

Footsteps Back to Primal

Footsteps Back to Primal

We're on the verge of something special here in the twenty-first century. The modern world is fertile with innovation. Advances in technology and medicine progress exponentially every day, changing the world before our eyes. Despite the fear mongering in the media, humans live longer and generally safer lives than any era in history. Our survival process is better organized than ever before. The number of people starving to death decreases every day thanks to an increasingly complex system of global food distribution, and more people die from suicide than they do of war and disease. Aside from the general memes of mainstream consumerism, humans want for nothing that they actually *need* in the modern world. The average human has more modern conveniences than royalty would have had a thousand years ago. And the richest among us live like the gods.

As I'm writing, I'm sitting in a café in California. Should I invest in the plane ticket, however, I can be in South Africa, Bali, or Hawaii by tomorrow. A mere century ago, I'd have booked a voyage by boat. Depending on where I am on the globe, it could have taken up to three months to reach my destination. At the touch of a button, a car appears at my house to take me wherever I'd like to go. Through the Internet, I debate the thoughts of the greatest philosophers and scientists, study music with the greatest musicians, and network faster than ever possible with my peers. A broken bone or bad infection used to mean a death sentence, depending on where you were living. Now, thanks to medicine, you'll be down for only a few weeks. And this is only the beginning.

In the next twenty years, AI and nano technology will revolutionize virtually every industry in existence, while the block-chain technology could very well render fiat currency obsolete. You only have to pay attention for a moment to marvel at what we've been able to create through our global competition and cooperation as a species.

And Yet, There's Something Wrong

While humans live longer and safer lives, we are generally less healthy as a global community. Diabetes, heart disease, dementia, and cancer have risen to epidemic proportions while mental illnesses such as depression and anxiety loom like perennial ghouls in the background. We're more stressed out than ever, keeping up with our neighbor; and for those of us who manage to make it to the top of the social hierarchy, we find that we're simply not as happy or fulfilled as we thought we would be. Indeed, there's no shortage of Hollywood stars, famed musicians, and celebrated writers, not to mention business tycoons who have taken the rope or put a gun to their heads. How can this be? They had everything…didn't they?

I offer a different view: that agrarian civilization came with radical changes in human behavior, and these changes are the source of our collective sickness and neurosis. Nine out of ten of the top killer-diseases are caused by how and what we eat, the environment we live in, the way we move, and even the way we socialize and have sex.

We're a hominid species with two hundred thousand years of hunter-gatherer history. Agriculture only occurred around ten thousand years ago, meaning that ninety-five percent of our history has been spent living in small, hunter-gatherer tribes of less than a few hundred people; hunting, foraging, and fishing for food and living very close to a natural environment.

With the advent of agriculture, all of this changed dramatically. Though agriculture is a recent development on the timeline, it rapidly reshaped how humans live and behave in many ways that are fundamental to our health. As we'll see in later chapters, how we connect with nature, how we eat, how we move, how we socialize, and how we have sex have all become inverted, thus constituting a behavioral revolution within the human species.

"Revolutions are dangerous," said the psychoanalyst Jordan Peterson in reference to social and political evolution. "People die." It's an incredibly difficult thing in general to get a good outcome. It's even more difficult, if not impossible, to get *rapidly-made, good outcomes for underbody*.

So what is the outcome of so rapid a change on a hominid body with millions of years of evolution behind its' design?

In the United States alone, over one hundred million people are pre-diabetic. Thirty million have heart disease, while the various forms of cancer plague over ten million. And despite what your physician tells you, these are <u>not</u> diseases typical of the human species. You'll rarely, if ever, find them among foraging tribes.

These diseases have been created by the conditions of civilization and the lifestyles that we adopted as agrarian societies progressed throughout the millennia: We box ourselves into Euclidian-shaped office spaces that would never be found in a natural environment; we eat over-processed, softened foods that offer scant nutritional value and allow our faces and jaws to become under-developed; we spend most of our time in sedentary positions for our work and entertainment; our social circles are shallow and ever-changing, and because of this, the sex we have (if we're getting any at all) is usually superficial and devoid of any real connection to our partners.

Thus, we begin to understand the healthcare crisis. Regarding the vast systems we have in place to keep us comfortable - as history has always indicated, what is built up so extravagantly can so often become rubble. Upon closer inspection, our modern society is a beautiful, albeit *fragile* house of cards. Where shall we be then when it inevitably crashes down?

Misguided by false views of hunter-gatherer life, we've been led to believe that we've reached the pinnacle of human existence and that we're the luckiest and most comfortable generation of humans. Debates rage on as to whether we're lucky, but we are certainly more comfortable, and this is part of the problem. Comfort is a blade that cuts both ways, and according to the statistics, it is currently gutting us. Many of the biological mechanisms that keep us healthy *only occur* when we're exposed to discomfort.

Examining our Roots

Like all life on earth, humans are a product of natural selection, and natural selection is the story of evolution. Time decides that you will evolve by way of DNA, which plays the role as a sort of biological blueprint. The human DNA is broken up into two parts: the genome, which stores information about your concrete traits such as skin and hair color, and general physical disposition such as height and weight. This part of your DNA accounts for about five percent and is generally concrete. Aside from plastic surgery, there's not much you can do to change it.

The epigenome, in contrast, is fluid and in constant flux. Even as you read this passage, your gene expression is changing based on the thoughts you're thinking, the quality of air you're breathing, the food you've eaten, and how much sleep you've had, as well as your level of fitness. You couldn't evolve at all if this were not the case.

Over time, based on your behavior and life-style, these gene expressions become slightly more concrete, leading to a more consistent pattern of expression. The blueprint becomes revised to reflect these changes, which then translate to physiological and anatomical modes of operation within the organism.

Multiply the timeframe to hundreds to thousands of years, and you begin to see a more permanent and cemented gene expression along with the characteristics that follow within a given population.

Then comes environment, which traditionally has decided *how* you will evolve. For example, if your tribe lives near a river-source, teeming with food, you and the group will become adept at living around that source of sustenance. Skills relatable to that environment will become more rewarded amongst the tribe, and thus more pronounced within the populace as a whole. Perhaps the environment calls for good swimmers and boat builders. Generations will pass, and you will begin to see the tribe develop characteristics such as these, because they, in turn, lead to survival of the whole group. You see the same thing throughout the animal kingdom.

You'll rarely find a species that isn't well-suited to its' environment, and the most well-adapted species present will be king of *that* environment. Time dictates that you will inevitably evolve. Environment dictates *how* you will evolve. Then come human beings. Here's where things get interesting.

We are one of the few, if not the *only*, land-based mammal that has gradually spread to all corners of the globe, living in a very diverse range of environments throughout our expansion, from the savanna flat-lands of Africa, the tropical forests of the Amazon Basin, to the windswept ice of the Arctic. This means that we are incredibly diverse as a species, as anyone can observe walking through an international airport. And yet, while we differ in some areas, we are the same in others.

We look at modern foraging groups to see defining traits across the human narrative. They and their life-style are the best representation of how our species evolved. The oldest of homo-sapiens fossils date to around two-to-three hundred thousand years. For the majority of that time, we lived upon the African savanna, foraging and hunting for our survival. Then something happened seventy thousand years ago. Maybe it was increasing population density that spurred our ancestors to new lands, or just general boredom. Whatever the case may have been, we begin to see human fossils being deposited throughout the Eurasian continent during that time. Fifty thousand years ago finds our remains turn up in Indonesian and Australian landmasses. Finally, from twelve thousand years ago, we begin to see human fossils in South America – a mobile species indeed.

By ten thousand years ago, agriculture had been discovered in multiple parts of the world, mostly throughout Europe and the Middle East. Humans began cultivating the land, and civilizations grew around that cultivation. The tribe became the village, the village became the town, the towns linked together through trade unions forming cities, and cities eventually connected, giving way to entire regions of cooperation known as empires. Fast forward on this trajectory to the last five hundred years, and through scientific innovation, we've paved the way to what is rapidly becoming a globalized society, where what happens in Silicon Valley affects what happens in Bangalore. Strings pulled in New York City affect change in Tokyo. Despite what the media will tell you, the march of history can largely be seen as the march towards unification, and yet that unification has come with a price.

"Too big to fail" is about as good of an expectation as *"too many cuts to bleed."* We have found order and security as a species by creating bigger and bigger societies. We have more people around us, more food to go around, and more comforts shielding us from the elements. Life is good, right? Wrong. With each new aspect of security, we add another cut to the wild animal inside of us. And with each new cut, the wilderness inside of us bleeds out just a little bit more.

But Wait…

This is not a book damning civilization. There have been too many positive advancements throughout the last ten thousand years for such an idea to be reasonable. Are we to forsake the art of the Renaissance period or the discourse of the ancient Greeks? How about the development of writing? What about mapping the genome, cracking relativity, or the development of solar energy? Self-proclaimed health-nut that I am, I can't justify forsaking the advancements in science, philosophy, and art in the name of a healthier life for humans. The words you're currently reading were typed on a computer thinner than a note pad, while the writer was enjoying espresso shipped from the jungles of Brazil. The fact that I'm even educated enough to write a book, not to mention you being educated enough to read one, is thanks to our education system, which has become standard across the globe.

To demonize modernity is not the answer, nor is it feasible. If somehow, our population (currently almost eight billion strong) collectively decided to go back to a foraging lifestyle, the result would be the starvation of billions of people. The key to living a healthy life is to find a balance between the animal that we've evolved to be while hacking the modern world that we now inhabit. After understanding where we come from and what we currently have, it becomes clear that we humans in the modern world have a brilliant and unprecedented opportunity.

With the technology and systems that characterize the twenty-first century, we now have a third aspect of evolution:

choice. Who do you want to be? What group do you want to be a part of? What do you *want* your life to mean in the end?

Pre-agricultural humans, as well as most post-agriculture humans, were typically forced into their lifestyle and behavior by the surrounding environment. Modern humans, however, are under no such arrangement. At any given time, we can all try out different diets, movement regimes, and philosophical outlooks on life; each of which have a very big effect upon how our genes code and change. Modern humans can determine how they will evolve. For the first time in our history as a species, *we hold the reins.* It is now our prerogative to decide where this wagon is headed. You have a choice: you can evolve negatively or positively. If you're reading this book, chances are you're looking to go the positive direction.

The Conscious Ape

To be a human being in the modern world is a fantastic possibility, but it comes with a hidden danger. Our survival process is better organized than ever before, and this can either be a great help in our evolution or a horrible hinderance. Humans used to need one another for survival. We used to confront danger on a daily basis, and this had a very beneficial effect on how our genes coded, as well as taking care of any sense of purpose and direction in life. "Take care of the tribe," was the mantra of the day. You'd rarely have ever found a Paleolithic man or woman at the bottom of a beer or wine bottle, lamenting about how life just isn't panning out. Humans need a purpose. Take this away, and the human animal becomes neurotic and sick, eventually wasting away in an endless succession of days lived out compulsively.

Consciousness is the key. Ask yourself for a moment: can you spend an entire hour doing nothing? Can you sit in solitude and simply allow your thoughts to pass objectively? The answer is probably no, and this is a tragedy, for it means that the very thing that separates us from other animals is turning against us. The ability to simply *be* is in the same hand - the ability to direct your life. Once you can sit down and simply be with yourself, you can then create your life how *you want it*. You can craft your life as you see fit, not by the seemingly inescapable dictates of life itself.

Footsteps

Imagine that you were able to simulate the lifestyle of our hunter-gatherer ancestors. Imagine waking up in the morning to the sound of birds and flowing water, charging your cellular mitochondria with fresh air and sunlight, exercising in ways that you enjoy, being a part of an intimate community, having healthy, deeply gratifying sex with your partner(s), and sleeping soundly at night, all while leveraging the boons of civilization to *your* advantage. The ability to travel, leverage technology to hack your peak-biochemistry, and the ability to choose who you want to be close to are yours to control. Not only would you be more human, but you could become super human.

To walk the line between order and freedom is to exercise the wilderness within while harnessing the advantages of civilization. To find a happy marriage between our evolutionary roots and the modern world we inhabit is to not only return home, but to bring something of worth back to that home.

Footsteps back to primal means embracing the creature that we are, and the one that we evolved to be. It means seeing through the veneer of what humans *should be* and, instead, to dive into the deep sea of human experience that simply *is*, should you allow it to be. The words that follow are the footsteps back to primal. Enjoy the walk.

February 2020
Santa Barbara, California

Table of Contents

PART I:
The Foundational Stone

Nature

Below the Trees of Eden

If you're reading this book, chances are you were raised within the folds of Western society. Western culture includes Australia and New Zealand, all nations that are a part of the European union, as well as North America and most parts of South America. Characterized by a host of artistic, philosophical, literary, and legal themes and traditions, Western culture also sports a commonly held belief: that we as a species have been *separated* from nature.

Every culture is the product of some religious outlook, and every religious outlook establishes what are called first principles.

First principles usually refer to the laws of physics at the most basic level. When we work form first principles, we understand matter at the most basic form. Because we work from this base, we understand how to build machinery that works, how to build houses that last, and how to build boats that don't sink. You'll never see a plane built with steel, nor a boat built out of lead. The former would never leave the ground, while the latter would be found at the bottom of the sea.

Culturally, first principles provide the foundational stones by which everything begins, and they become the psychological basis of every citizen within the fold of a particular society.

A first principle of Western society is that mankind has been separated from nature. The origin of this belief can be traced back to the scriptures of the Judeo-Christian tradition, to the story of Adam and Eve.

The first humans had a pretty good life, according to the narrative. They lived in naked leisure, basking in the good graces of God, and they enjoyed a boundless supply of nourishing food. Sadly, it couldn't last. Having listened to the words of a clever serpent, Eve, the first woman, indulges in fruit from the tree of knowledge and becomes enlightened. Now, as you might expect, no enlightened woman is going to put up with an un-enlightened male. So with a new leafy skirt and some primitive form of the first Wonderbra, off she walks to tempt her male companion. Adam, the first man, succumbs to her earnest requests (as men often do), and the first couple are officially *awake*.

God doesn't like this too much, according to the story. Upon finding out, he gives an eloquent speech denouncing the serpent while banishing the humans to a life of sweat and sorrow. Childbirth becomes a painful affair, and humanity is said to have fallen from grace upon that day.

Whether you believe literally in the account or not is irrelevant. There is one fundamental truth embedded here: humans *have left the garden*. Until around ten thousand years ago humans lived predominantly in the wilderness. There were very few villages and towns, and there certainly were no cities. Our ancestors were spread across the globe clustered in a vast number of unique tribes, each with its' own local customs and traditions. Some tribes were peaceful, and others were war-like. Some lived in cold climates while others lived in tropical locales.

Regardless of the culture, gratitude towards the environment was a hallmark. Whether peace-loving or warlike towards *other human tribes*, each tribe viewed itself as the beneficiary of nature's boundless produce. The land gave these early humans all that they required and in return, there had to be in place a culturally enforced respect for the surrounding environment.

Years were spent observing nature, because this meant survival. The average hunter-gatherer even today has an immediate and intimate knowledge about their surrounding environment. The mere thought of damaging that which gives life would be unthinkable and severely punished by other members of the tribe. Among the Kung of the Kalahari Desert, for example, destruction of the environment would usually be punishable by death because it would theoretically symbolize a direct threat to the entire tribe. All of this changed, however, with the development of agriculture.

For the first time, humans began to set up more permanent villages and settlements in order to work the land. These permanent villages were the first steps towards placing walls between ourselves and the natural world. The most fundamental difference between foraging life, and agricultural life was a shift in mindset. Rather than seeing nature as an ally, we began to see the environment as something to *contend with*. Nature was no longer the bountiful produce of spring and leaves turning in autumn. It never rained enough, sometimes it rained too much, a sudden cold-spell could spell disaster, and pests were always invading the crop that you did manage to grow. The life of a farmer even today is no easy affair.

Should the successful farmer pull off the harvest, there was rarely extra food left over because of the resulting population booms. Foragers would often space their children out for at least three or four years so that the children can learn to walk and become somewhat independent. This makes sense for a community that stays mobile. The settlers, however, were under no such dictate. The now-sedentary woman could give birth each year if she chose to do so. The population booms effectively closed the gate behind us. We could no longer support an expanding population through the hunter-gatherer lifestyle. In many ways, agriculture was a trap.

As we became more sedentary and less aware of the environment, nature became the enemy. Throughout the passing of generations, rather than understanding our environment, we became more adept at placing barriers between us and the vengeful goddess. The settlement became the village, the village became the city, the city became the empire, and the empire became the nation-state, until we arrive at present day where we are becoming an increasingly unified global society. Something that takes place in Bangalore affects what happens in Silicon Valley. Each step has gradually led us further away from the roots that nourish us, and it didn't take long before a very real fear of nature became common.

It's important to remember that the Judeo-Christian ethics

didn't begin this type of pathology. Agriculture is at least twelve thousand years old, while the authors of Genesis didn't pen their thoughts until around thirty-five hundred years ago. The significance here is not that that the first principles of the Judeo-Christian system began the mindset shift, but only that it rationalized and *validated* it. I selected the Judeo-Christian ethics to pick upon only because I'm most familiar with them as an American.

According to the world economic forum, fifty-six percent of the human population live in cities. Among these people, an increasing number have never stepped foot in the woods, nor paddled out into the sea. Many don't know where their food actually comes from, nor how their products and resources are produced.

Funny as it may be to those who grew up in the countryside, there's a stark reality here: separate a tree from its roots and it will eventually die altogether. In the case of humans, our collective neurosis and the growing cases of preventable disease, not to mention our insatiable desire to dominate and destroy the environment, are but the dying pains of our slowly unraveling defeat as a species. You'll find no better place to witness these dying pains than the nervous system.

The nervous system consists of the brain, the spine, and the miles of nerve endings that communicate to each cell of the body. It governs how we learn, how we carry out our work, how we digest food, how we sleep, how we have sex, and ultimately, how we feel. By way of the autonomic nervous system, it ultimately has top-down control of the entire body. Herein lies the modern conundrum facing every modern human.

Your Nervous System Comes with Expectations

Imagine that you're a soccer player and you train for a year for your debut. You go through all the motions, learning to kick and dribble, tackle and evade, and pass and sprint, honing your body and brain to the patterns of the game. Then, imagine on game day that your coach hands you a golf club. "Hit par, or you're out," he says. There's no reason to think you'd succeed. Likewise, there's no reason to believe that the human body can thrive in our current environment.

To be short, our nervous systems evolved for a certain "game." Having evolved for eons within nature, your brain comes with certain expectations. The auditory region of the brain is expecting the sounds of bird-call, wind, and water. Your nose is expecting the scent of natural aerosols from surrounding vegetation, and the occasional scat of predator and prey, while your visual system is expecting the fractal-patterned landscape of the forest, the savanna, the mountains, and the sea. This is the "game" we evolved to play.

Instead, the modern human plays a game of alarm clocks, traffic noise, the scent of gasoline fumes, angry clientele, bills piled to the ceiling, and the sight of Euclidian-shaped infrastructure. In addition, with the rise of technology and our inability to use it responsibly, each of us are bombarded with far more information per day than our nervous systems are meant to process. One has to ask, "What are the effects of so drastic a change?" From a perspective of the nervous system, we see one thing: stress.

A Modern Scourge

We wake up to it at the dawn's first reveille and wade through it until we finally lay our weary heads to sleep (if we ever do at all.) Stress has been called the scourge of the modern world. One-third of Americans admit to dealing with extreme stress, defined as being on the verge of a mental break-down, while nearly half of all Americans report feeling stressed throughout the day.

Stress is caused by environmental stimuli and acts as a warning bell. It wasn't too long ago that our stress response stood between us and death. When something occurs that literally threatens your survival, your brain responds with a release of cortisol, creating a chain reaction of physiological events that throw you into a fight-or-flight response.

Imagine that you're driving down the road and the car next to you suddenly swerves in front of you. In a split second, you slam on the breaks to avoid collision and watch the driver speed on down the road oblivious to the close call they created. Your heart rate is up along with your middle finger, and you're breathing hard, possibly even sweating. That's stress. It's the same mechanism that would take place if you were out on the savanna and spotted a hungry-looking lion. Stress says, "Pay attention to *that* dumbass!" And because you pay attention and act, you survive.

The problem in the modern world is that we deal with far too much stimuli, and our nervous systems are sprinting to keep up. On a hike in the woods, the vast majority of your time will be spent gazing at the natural scenery around you. Perhaps you'll even sit on a stump somewhere and allow your mind to drift. A seasoned hiker can expect to run into wildlife every now and then, such as a bear or mountain lion, which will cause a high-stress response. This is normal. What isn't normal, however, is to have *multiple* high-stress events each day.

A person living in the modern world will run into more "lions" in one morning driving to work than a forager would have in a whole day in the bush. But it doesn't stop there. Now you're at work. You've missed a deadline and your boss is on your tail. Your job security is in question. Perhaps your marriage is falling apart. You're over-extended financially, and you have few, if any, savings. If you became sick and couldn't work, your living arrangement would be in question in a matter of months. God forbid you have children (which you probably do). Now their survival is in question as well because of your ineptitude. Welcome to the life of the average Westerner. The lions might be locked up in the local zoo, but the real threat is those that exist in your mind. Drip, drip, drip retorts the cortisol, like the merciless beat of a drum. Enter chronic stress, where your body and brain become trapped in a gradual release of cortisol, thus keeping you in a consistent pattern of fight-or-flight. To understand why this is so deadly, we must first understand the system that makes all of this possible.

Your stress response, known as your sympathetic response, is but one-half of your autonomic nervous system. The other half is called *para*-sympathetic. In contrast to the fight-or-flight sympathetic response, your para-sympathetic is your "rest and digest" system. This is where you can relax, watch a movie, read a book, have sex, digest food, perform excretion, and ultimately **sleep**.

When the body is caught in a constant fight-or-flight response, it can't carry out these normal functions that are crucial to our health, thus beginning a vicious cycle that will slowly leave you withered..

It typically starts off with a bad night's sleep. You arrive home after a stressful day. You're cranky and wired. You lay your head down, close your eyes, but your mind won't stop. You spend the night tossing and turning, dreading the morning to come. You trudge to work for another day of the grind, but with a new twist. Because you didn't sleep, the ratio between your leptin and ghrelin levels are off. A healthy balance of leptin and ghrelin will insure satiety when eating. When they are out of balance, you begin to have cravings, especially for sugar. You eat a few donuts on the way to work and chase it with increasing amounts of coffee. Thus begins the sugar roller coaster, along with caffeine addiction. Your sugar spikes, causing the release of insulin. Sugar is shuttled into the cells, causing an overshoot, leading to hypoglycemia or low blood sugar. Once this happens, you want more sugar. To survive the day, you binge caffeine and return home to have trouble sleeping yet again. Weeks turn into months, and months turn into years as the cycle repeats itself over and over again. Maybe it's not a problem if it happens to one person but what about ten? What about one hundred? A million? Even worse, what if it's the way of an entire *culture?* It's common belief, for example, in Western society that you have a harder time sleeping as you age. Is it? Or is it the fact that along with the many gifts we've been given in Western society, we've also inherited a few bad habits? As we live out those bad habits over time, the problems become bigger and more threatening. Furthermore, what happens when our bad habits are monetized?

Take a look a look around you: there's a billion dollar industry surrounding sugar and caffeine addictions alone. Add to that medications for anxiety, depression, heart disease, and diabetes, and you begin to see the bigger picture. The stressors of modern society create problems in the body which we (partially) solve with medication. ADHD? Have some Ritalin. Diabetes? Have some insulin with an extra shot of metformin. How about your anxiety and depression? We've got you covered with some fucking trazodone.

You pop a pill to solve one problem while creating two or three others. The following list is considered "minor" side effects of general prescription pills.

- Diarrhea/constipation
- Dizziness
- Drowsiness
- Fatigue
- Heart issues (palpitations, irregular heartbeats)
- Hives
- Nausea and vomiting
- Rash
- Stomach upset
- Trouble sleeping
- Nose bleed
- Headaches
- <u>Low libido</u>

I underlined the last one for a reason. Call me crass at twenty-seven years of age, but if a list of potential side-effects includes *lowering* my ability to pursue and have sex, I'm trotting like hell from whatever causes that "minor" symptom. And yet this is considered normal in modern society - a simple reality of growing older.

We have an entire culture formed around protecting the bad habits that eventually kill us. Why? Why not just remove the problems? Furthermore, you might call it naïve for proposing that a simple walk through the woods can provide you with all the benefits of your daily pill. I'll show you why you're wrong.

Shinrin Yoku: The Art of Forest Bathing

Just as the first principles of the West trace their roots back to a separation from nature, far-Eastern culture can trace its' roots back to a direct opposite. Nature is within us, according to the Eastern philosophy. Modern-day Japan finds itself placed along the intersection of two of these cooperating ideologies: Shinto and Buddhism.

Shinto belief revolves around the idea that everything has kami, or spirit. Every animal, tree, rock, and even every sound wave are imbued with presence of the divine. Meanwhile, the core teachings of Buddhism revolve around a man who abandoned a life of material comfort to find enlightenment in, of all places, the forest.

First principles don't necessarily dictate every move a society makes. Despite such a nature-infused ideology, Japan has a long history of working it's population to death. Torn between the wisdom of the past and the necessity of being a player in the global economy, the country has produced one of the hardest-working cultures in the world, founded upon a wide-spread culture of rice cultivation. "In order to be a successful rice farmer," writes Malcom Gladwell, "you have to rise every morning before dawn, and work in many cases past dusk." In addition, Japan spent thousands of years immersed in the Bushido culture of the Samurai, a breed of warrior whose highest aim was an honorable death in service to a master. In such a society, only the grittiest, most dedicated workers would find success, even if it meant their own demise.

Translate this grit and determination (and a profound disregard for personal safety) to a globalized society and you have a country that routinely outperforms others in academics, produces ferocious soldiers (as we learned the hard way in WW2), and a labor-force dedicated to service of a superior, all while being willing to literally die doing so. Since the 1980s, "karoshi," or death from overwork, has been a common term among the Japanese lexicon, and for the citizens who just can't cope with the culture, the country currently boasts the third highest suicide rate in the world, behind South Korea and Hungary.

When you have a problem, you use first principles as the basis for solving them. Increasingly burdened by the toll modern life has on their population, the Japanese government turned back to nature. Shinrin Yoku, the art of forest bathing, was unearthed and re-examined.

Forest bathing is the act of allowing nature through all the senses. The philosophy holds that the five senses are windows, corridors by which the world around us enters our being.

Your sight is how you distinguish objects within a visually complex environment, which fruits are edible, which are poisonous, whether there are predator or prey within your environment, and so on. Your ability to hear allows you to triangulate the position of predators and prey, and your sense of smell, perhaps your most primal, can help you detect unseen and unheard threats. The most primal of the senses, your smell has a direct pathway to the brain, bypassing the blood/brain barrier altogether.

Interesting things happen when we allow nature through these corridors. Within minutes of walking into the woods, your breathing will slow, and the cortisol levels will lower in your body. After an hour, you'll have a better attention span and your ability to solve complex problems will increase. After three days in the wilderness, the pre-frontal cortex relaxes and your ability for creativity will sky-rocket by over fifty percent.

For centuries, nature-writers like Muir and Thoreau advised the public to spend more of our time in nature, though they didn't have the scientific data to back up their claims. They were nonetheless aware of the increasing gap between the technology-driven world of production and efficiency and the natural world of rhythm and unity. Nature only moves as fast as is required, while human civilization repeatedly sacrifices human well-being at the altar of rapid progression and growth. We create technology that allows us to do our work more efficiently and instead of scaling back and allowing the technology to do the work, we instead do <u>more</u> with the same amount of time.

In the documentary, *How Much Time Does Time Have?* the average modern human being does more work than a forager could ever expect to or want to do. We get a lot done, sure. But is it good for us? Are we happy and more fulfilled? Or do we eventually realize that we're worn out cogs in the machine?

The More We Do, The More Shallow We Become

By leveraging the processing power of technology, we've increased our work load ten-fold. It used to take weeks, even months to contact others over long-distance, and then just as long to receive a reply. Compare that to a day at the office, and you can contact friends, family, and work associates within seconds via email. Often times, these people expect a direct reply within minutes.

All this activity leaves us feeling empty, shallow, and neurotic. We've lost the ability to simply do nothing and be at peace. We've lost the ability to sit and connect with our inner depths. The more shallow we become, the less color life seems to have. Because we've lost the ability to zone out, crucial parts of our brain are becoming unbalanced. This is where nature comes to the rescue.

Natural environments are immediately recognized by our nervous systems, meaning that our brains can be fully engaged in nature while also being able to relax. To get an understanding of this, we'll look at the three main networks of the brain, and the significance of their interplay.

Networks of the Brain, and The Art of Non-Doing

Our brain navigates any environment through the function of three main networks. The executive network is our problem solving mechanism. Housing the pre-frontal cortex, our ability for higher reasoning and intellectuality is found here. When you're reading or writing a book, doing math, or changing a flat tire, seducing somebody, or presenting a proposal to your boss, you're utilizing this network.

Our spatial network is how we orient to our environment. Rooted in the parietal lobe, it is what allows us to experience the world in a subjective way and why you can navigate an environment without bumping into things.

Then there is the default network. Viewed widely as the lazy brother to the executive network, not to mention the bane of every micro-managing boss, this could best be termed as our day-dreaming mode. Those moments when you simply zone out and think of nothing find you here. Society has taught us that these moments are a waste, limiting our productivity and therefore our ability to affect change in the world. The reality is the opposite.

By zoning out, we allow the chatty prefrontal cortex to finally relax. We can let our minds go. The Taoists called this place the void – a place of emptiness and peace within every human mind. Coincidentally, the default network is where poetry, music, and art come from.

In the modern world, the executive network is praised, and it's very easy to see why. This is what allows us to cut through our objectives for the day. It's what finishes tasks and keeps you at work late at night in order to meet deadlines. Without it, you'd be fired tomorrow for your incapacity to do your work. The executive network is the sword that cuts through the work of life. But every sword needs sharpened, lest it become dull. Inside every modern human being is a flagging executive network. This is exactly where the default network steps in.

Ideally, the executive and default operate in tandem. When the executive network becomes fatigued, the default network can step in, allowing the executive to rest up for another round in the arena. When you allow yourself time to zone out, you find that you become much more effective in getting things done, and with much less stress.

The hustle-and-bustle mentality associated with getting more things accomplished is backwards. People are overworked in modern society. The blade has gone blunt. Instead of allowing our minds to rest, we search for increasingly destructive ways to continue cutting. Caffeine is one way that we do this. Some even go as far as a cocaine addiction. There's no reason for this. We can be much more effective simply by taking a walk in our local park and letting nature through the windows.

The Foundational Stone

Every temple needs a foundational stone before it can rise to the sky. Allowing nature into our lives is not only a healthy hack, but a necessity.

Let me be clear: the rules of this book begin with hacking your environment because your environment is where you spend most of your time, whether it be your home or workspace. Allowing nature into our lives is the foundational stone by which we build our temple. The chapters that follow will be helpful, yes, but without a healthy environment, they will be like seeds planted in a soil bereft of nutrients. You can have the perfect diet, a good movement routine, a healthy social network, and plenty of sex. If you are in a chronically stressed out state, it will mean little.

For those of us who live out in the woods, allowing nature into your life is as simple as walking out your front door. For those in the city environments, here are a few modern hacks that you can use to bring the wilderness into your home.

Bush craft: deeply embedded within every human is an instinct to survive. Amazing things happen when you exercise these instincts. There are courses all around the world where you can go and safely learn survival craft out in the woods. Knowing how to make a fire out of scratch, how to find food in the woods, and how to build a shelter are incredibly practical skills that apply to many different aspects of life. Learn these skills, take them out, and put them to the test. My favorite times in life have been when I was camping out on a beach or in the woods somewhere with a close group of friends. Eating food gathered from the environment, drinking water fresh from a mountain stream, making love bathed in the light of the campfire, surrounded by the sounds of the wilderness. That's the good shit. Go get some of it. But for the love of God, please don't be reckless. Take a course, learn the skills, dip your toes. We can't all be Bear Grylls after a single day.

Local parks: short of an all-out camping trip, humans need to find time in the trees. If you live in a city or town, get creative. Take your lunch break in the local park. Sit by a river stream and allow your thoughts to flow like the river. If you live by the sea, make walks a part of your daily routine.

Indoor plants: there's overwhelming evidence that house plants will greatly improve your environment. Visually, they will help stimulate the nervous system in a relaxing way due to the fractal patterns of the leaves and vines. They also filter pollutants out of the air. Many of your common house plants have shown the ability to absorb toxic substances such as formaldehyde, benzene, and trichloroethylene. In addition, they absorb excess CO2 out of the environment while also pumping out fresh oxygen, creating a better environment that your respiratory system will thank you for.

Essential oils: your sense of smell elicits an immediate physiological response. You can game this by using certain scents. Essential oils are concentrated liquids from various plants. Depending on the type, they can be applied directly to the skin, ingested orally, or diffused into the air. By diffusing them into the air of your home, you can hack you physiology through your sense of smell. Smell is the most primal of the human senses, and can elicit an immediate physiological response.

Smells of citrus tend to energize the body, while scents from lavender, rosemary, and sandalwood have a calming effect on the nervous system. Diffuse certain oils at specific times of the day, and watch as they allow you to settle into the mode of being that you want.

Wind, water, and bird call: these are the sounds that we evolved alongside, and they have an immediate effect upon our nervous system. There are awesome resources for this online. Spotify, YouTube, and Pandora are great examples. As I'm writing, a YouTube video is playing the sound of rain falling on a roof while a piano echoes in the distance.

Letting the cold in: allowing your body to be cold once a day is a powerful healing factor. It's been shown that within ten days, a cold shower for up to a minute will show positive results in the efficiency of your vascular system.

Adopt an animal: pets come with a plethora of benefits. They'll keep you active throughout the day while showing you unconditional love and companionship. Caring for an animal has been shown to release neuro-chemicals such as dopamine and oxytocin.

We can't go back to the wilderness completely, but we can begin our journey back by bringing the wilderness to us. By hacking our environment in the twenty-first century, we can begin to pave the way back to our primal roots.

PART II
Energy

All life is a form of movement. Show me a river with torrents raging, and I will declare that a healthy river. Show me a shallow, stagnant pool with leaves trapped in the corners, and I will point to the origin of disease. There is a river system within every human being. The next two chapters will explore how to keep it flowing.

MOVEMENT

A Body in Motion

The nature of life itself is that of perennial movement and flux. Break down any physical object to its most basic component, the atom, and you'll find a nucleus comprised of a proton and neutron, as well as an electron circling the pair in eternal dance. What is interesting is that if you take the electron away, the entire atom will become unstable and fall apart. Had this happened at the dawn of time, chemistry itself wouldn't have been possible, there would be no element, and life could not exist.

All physical bodies, from the atomic to the cosmic, exist in a state of movement. Pulled by gravity, each object cycles around another that is bigger. Like this, the electron circles the proton and neutron, our moon circles planet Earth, and we on planet Earth cycle around the sun. Our sun, along with the entire solar system, cycles ever deeper into the Milky Way galaxy. Indeed, even our galaxy is subject to the gravitational pull of other galaxies surrounding it.

On Earth we see cycles in the form of rivers carving a path to the sea, while in the ocean we find them in the massive gyro systems that circle every major coastline. In the human body we see a similar river-like pattern comprising the miles of veins, arteries, and blood vessels that spread from our heads to our toes.

Movement is what keeps a body healthy, from the smallest of quarks to the monolith star. Without movement, the earth itself would stagnate, and life would cease to exist.

The Sedentary Ape

While the rest of physical existence remains in its natural dance, humans have taken a one hundred and eighty degree turn. Prior to agriculture, humans typically moved with the seasons, living in nomadic tribes, moving from one camp to another. When they were settled into a particular camp, hours a day were spent searching for food.

Agriculture demanded the exact opposite. Dealing with crops meant establishing more permanent settlements where we could drive off the invading animals, and establish food storage centers for the boon that was created by working the land. Humans slowly, generation after generation, became more sedentary as a species.

When we did move, it was in ways that were directly opposite to what we've evolved for. When you look at the anatomical structure of the body, you see a form that is made for movements that require lengthening and stretching of the frame, such as running and climbing. Farming and gardening on the other hand, involve movements like bending over and picking up heavy objects, swinging hammers, hoes, and axes. These movements compress the spine and joints and are hell on the body in the long run.

Such movements and the resulting injuries very well could have necessitated the development of technology that could act as mechanical leverage. It took a few thousand years, but eventually "smarter, not harder," became the common mantra, and the post-agriculture style of hard work became something to be feared and even ridiculed among social elites.

Our foraging ancestors didn't have a choice but to move. Grocery stores didn't exist. Food was *out there* and needed to be brought back. They hiked, climbed, swam, hunted, and foraged. This diversity of movement is reflected in our anatomy and is even thought to be one of the reasons we evolved such complex brains. Humans are not exactly stellar physical specimens. Usain Bolt will never out run a cheetah, and our most accomplished strong man would be destroyed by the average chimpanzee. Humans have thrived nonetheless because of our ability to move in diverse ways throughout a constantly changing environment. Very few animals can run, climb, and swim and do all of them efficiently. The human machine is truly special in this regard.

Fast forward to today's world where everything is technology driven, and it's very easy to forget that we *need* to move. We've effectively engineered the need for movement out of virtually every part of our society, thus removing the necessity to do so. Your average urbanite wakes up, commutes an hour to work by car, sits at a desk for eight hours, and commutes back home. The food is at the grocery store, and if you're feeling lazy, have no fear. Even more rural places can enjoy Uber Eats nowadays, while Amazon actually delivers groceries. It's certainly an easy life in the modern world, but is it healthy?

The parts of our brain that separate us from animals, the cortex, only evolved upon the foundation of our motor function. Movement and higher cerebral function go hand in hand, as we'll soon see. By taking movement out of our daily routine, we are degrading the parts of our brains that separate us from more primitive forms of life. And as we're about to see, there are consequences - the main of which is that we might lose our ability to move entirely. And then where shall our minds be?

Move It or Lose It

A central theme of evolution is efficiency. The body will not manufacture that which it doesn't see a need for. From an evolutionary perspective, this is on point. Economically, to maintain a body is no frugal affair. Muscle, for example, is very expensive. It requires a higher metabolic rate and increased fat burn to maintain. If the body doesn't foresee a requirement for it, say, to move weight, sprint, swim, climb, or perform even a moderate level of physical activity, it simply won't put the required infrastructure in place, and you will lose the ability to move altogether. The same is true for your cerebral function and your circulatory system. Once that happens, you'll spend your days wasting away in palliative care, an industry, by the way, that boasts an annual revenue of thirty-three billion dollars and will only continue to grow as human health worsens worldwide.

"Movement" is much more than swinging a kettle bell, doing pull ups, or running long distance. What are you moving? Are you moving blood and lymph? Are you tearing apart muscle fibers? Are you merely trying to move nutrients in order to heal? Movement has a major effect on virtually every system of the body, but for this chapter we'll stay with three parts: the respiratory system, the vascular system, and the brain. To start off, we'll begin with the most basic and perhaps the most important movement in the body - energy.

If you've ever been to a yoga class, chances are you've heard the word "prana." Simply put, prana is the "life force" or "vital energy." The more prana and organism has, the more alive it is. This concept was first developed three thousand years ago in the Indian and Chinese cultures of antiquity, and from there the medicinal concept spread. In China, it was known as Ch'i while the Japanese called it "Ki." The Greeks knew it as "pneuma," while the American Indians knew it as "orenda."

Each of these cultures developed ways to keep the life force flowing throughout the human body. Those who failed to keep the energy flowing met an untimely death. The Chinese developed Qigong, the Hindus developed the practice of Yoga, and the Iroquois developed the Orena system of breathing.

Health within the human body is about renewing and moving this vital energy, allowing it to flow and nourish the cells. Imagine that within your body there exists a river-system that transports everything from blood, nutrients, neuro-transmitters, and hormones, as well as flushes out toxins and waste. You would say that a rushing river is better than a stagnant pool, and that's exactly the point. You want your river system flowing.

By failing to move, you allow the river to go stagnant. Still water breeds poison, and this is a major cause for disease in the modern world. While it's difficult to prescribe any particular movement for human beings, one thing is certain. You can't go wrong by breathing.

Breathe

Thanks to enthusiasts like Whom Hoff, science is beginning to prove what the ancients knew all along – that life starts with the breath. Breathing is the most powerful way to move energy throughout the body. You can have the perfect diet and a good exercise routine, but if you're not breathing fully, you simply won't be as effective in what you're doing. The average human takes around twenty thousand breaths per day. Depending on how you take them, whether fast or slow, through your mouth or nose, your bio-chemistry reflects a certain degree of health.

It's ironic then that we take this for granted. Think about it - if I take food away from you, you'll last for weeks as long as you have water. That's called fasting. If I take water away from you, it'll take around three to five days for you to perish of thirst. Now imagine if I take your oxygen away. Five minutes under and brain cells begin to die. Ten minutes and you'll likely suffer a coma and permanent brain damage. Over fifteen minutes and you're dead. Beyond ten minutes, and you probably wouldn't want to continue living anyways.

Oxygen is a necessity down to the cellular level, but this wasn't always the case for life on Earth. Quite the opposite. The first life appeared on Earth about four billion years ago, and it was comprised primarily of prokaryotic, single-celled organisms. These guys disdained oxygen and breathed carbon-dioxide instead which was then very plentiful, while the waste-product created was oxygen. Then, two and a half billion years ago came a different kind of life: the multi-celled eukaryote. Comprised of multiple prokaryotes, the eukaryotes were different in that they used the previously discarded oxygen as fuel. This would prove to be an important step in the evolutionary process. It turns out that oxygen respiration yields sixteen times more energy production than that of carbon-dioxide. With all the extra energy to go around, a new threshold of evolutionary possibility was realized, and more complex life-forms were the result.

Virtually, all complex life that we see today, from plants to animals are forms of eukaryotes. Humans themselves are a mere extension of this evolutionary pathway. Your body is comprised of hundreds of billions of eukaryotic cells, and each one of them require oxygen to thrive. When you stunt your breathing, you starve them of that life, and this is the root of many diseases that plague humanity.

Hunter-gatherers don't have to remember to do breathing exercises. Moving the body requires energy, and they move a lot throughout the day, sometimes very strenuously. As they labor, their breath labors as well, and this keeps their vascular system strong and healthy.

Western society, for the most part, has only observed the power of breathing to a limited extent. According to current medical analysis, it matters little whether you breathe through your nose or through your mouth. Fast or slow, full or shallow? What's the difference? And yet, one quick look at our anatomy will show how flawed such thinking is.

The respiratory muscles include the nasal concha, larynx, diaphragm, the intercostals between the ribs, the abs, and the muscles of the neck. All in all, these muscles account for ten to twelve percent of your muscle mass depending on your size. That's a lot! And just like all other muscles, they atrophy without use. If your "beach body" muscles atrophy, it's not the end of the world. You can still live a reasonably healthy life. But if your breathing muscles atrophy, you've got a problem.

Altogether, one billion people worldwide suffer from some form of respiratory condition. Bronchitis, asthma, pneumonia, emphysema, or lung cancer, the single common denominator is always lack of the ability to breathe. While the prevailing belief in Western medicine is that the nose is but a ancillary organ and otherwise irrelevant to your health and quality of life, nothing can be further from the truth.

Breathing and the Autonomic Nervous System

Stress is perhaps the most wide-spread ailment people suffer from, and yet it doesn't have to be that way. If you are stressed, it simply means you are not *in control* of your stress response.

The world doesn't control your stress levels. You do through *how* you use your breath. This is no secret. Various high-performing individuals, from Olympic athletes to Navy SEALs, have been honing the powers of the breath for hundreds of years.

The lungs are covered in nerves which are connected into both parts of the autonomic nervous system. You'll remember from chapter one that your sympathetic nervous system controls your fight-or-flight while the para-sympathetic controls your rest-and digest state. Depending on how you're breathing, you shift your body into one of the two.

Short and shallow breathing leads to a stressed state. This is caused by nerves in the upper lobes of the lungs that directly connect to your sympathetic response. When you breathe rapidly, you stimulate these nerves, which then signal your brain to release cortisol and adrenaline, thus creating a fight-or-flight state. As you move deeper into the lower lobes of the lungs, you see nerves that are connected to the para-sympathetic nervous system. As you breathe deeper and slower cycles, air moves further down into the lungs and your para-sympathetic nerves become activated, thus signaling the body to relax. By stimulating these nerves, you can keep your body relatively relaxed, and you can even access deeper states of meditation.

It certainly pays to add breathing exercises into your daily routine, but for this book, we will keep it simple. Breathe through your nose, breathe deeply, and slow it down. You'll feel more energy and more clarity throughout your day, and you'll limit the release of runaway cortisol, allowing you to keep a lid on your stress.

Getting Cerebral: Movement and the Brain

Humans are puny wimps compared to other animals. The smallest chimp would make short work of us physically, while even a honey badger would tear us to shreds in most confrontations. What truly sets us apart from the animal kingdom is the organ between our ears.

The brain is comprised of over one hundred billion neurons, each of which communicate to the others by way of hundreds of different neurotransmitters. Even though the brain takes up a mere six to seven percent of the body's weight, it uses over twenty-five percent of the body's energy, making it by far the most expensive weapon in our arsenal. Why such a cost?

Humans don't stand much of a chance physically, but our ability to outwit and outlearn our competitors is unmatched. One human can't kill a mammoth, but the mammoth stands no chance against a dozen of us armed with heavy spears and a hunting strategy. Our ability to collectively outwit other creatures has been the master key to our domination of the globe. As we'll see, movement and learning go hand in hand. You cannot have one without the other

Making Connections

Learning requires the strengthening of connections between circuited neurons. This is achieved through a mechanism known as long-term potentiation. In layman's terms, the more you study something over the long term, the better you (potentiate) learn it. We all know this. But how does it work?

The first time you study something such as a new language or mathematical formulae, existing nerve cells are recruited to form a new pathway, and a neurotransmitter known as glutamate is fired between the new pathway, much like how a plane barrels down a runway before takeoff. Each day, as you continue to study, signals of glutamate (more planes) continue to fire down the new pathway, requiring more space, thus making it wider and more developed. In this way, memories are developed and knowledge is born.

Glutamate is responsible for firing the signals between neurons to bring them closer together, but there is another neurotransmitter that comes in to build and strengthen the infrastructure. BDNF, or brain-derived neurotrophic factor, is responsible for this process of building the infrastructure of the new pathways while also maintaining those that already exist. Over five thousand scientific papers have been published on BDNF, making it one of the poster-children of neuroscience. The best way to generate BDNF in the brain is (you guessed it) by exercising.

When you exercise, you put the body under stress, and stress by definition is something that challenges the body in ways that it isn't prepared for. The brain, likened to the perfect student, responds to the perceived threat by assuming it doesn't know something about the world and that it needs to learn something in order to survive. So BDNF is up-regulated in order to bolster defenses related to the particular "threat." Let's say you go for a run with a friend and he's a better runner than you are. You spend the hour-long session heaving like a madman to get air and keep up, your heart rate spikes, and you can feel the cortisol buzzing in your head.

From your brain's perspective, this is not good. So it up-regulates BDNF in order to change the brain and the body to better survive the assault on your cardiovascular system. As the weeks go by, your VO2 max increases, and you develop running muscles in your legs, not to mention feel good neuro-chemicals that blunt the discomfort of the run. Glutamate and BDNF are the masterminds behind these changes. The added benefit is that you now have left over BDNF to pursue whatever vocation or subject you would like, and you will learn it faster. Whether you're learning a musical instrument, a mathematical formula, a language, or even a new way of thinking, it will help you to bolster your efforts with BDNF. So go for a walk, go run, bang some iron, and watch your abilities to learn soar.

Exercise primes the brain to learn by inducing a feeling of euphoria and alertness, as everyone who's ever finished a distance run knows. Couple this with its ability to encourage nerve cells to bind together to form pathways, and you have a fertile ground by which to grow new brain cells.

Choosing Your Movement Type

Should you be a long distance runner or a climber? A CrossFit athlete, a soccer player, or a martial artist? The answer can honestly be all of the above. It all depends on what kind of brain you would like to have.

Maybe you're a book nerd or a language buff and you just want to prime your brain to learn new information. In this case, a little bit of aerobic exercise will be just fine. Just thirty minutes a day of aerobic exercise at seventy percent of your capacity has been shown to boost executive function and spur the development of BDNF in the brain.

If you have no aspirations to be a more dominant athlete, and you merely want to memorize information better, then aerobic work will get you there. The boosted executive function will allow you to tackle your tasks at hand, while the BDNF generated in the hippocampus will allow you to store new information and make new neuro-pathways. *Voila*, you're smarter!

For those who want to take the process further, many benefits to doing more than just aerobic exercise can be found, particularly when talking about movements that must be learned, such as karate, dancing, gymnastics, or surfing. The more complex the movement being learned, the more complex the synaptic connections throughout the brain.

Imagine the first time you learn something complicated, such as a dance routine. You stumble through the movement and you feel awkward. God forbid somebody you admire (or fancy) is watching. Now imagine it from your brain's standpoint. Parts like your cerebellum and basal ganglia wake up. These are where movement and motor function are concerned. Since you've never performed these movements, however, they have no idea what is going on. So they communicate to the hippocampus, where short-term learning is concerned "Pay attention!" they say. The hippocampus takes note and begins the process of learning the new pattern. As you continue to learn the dance each day, the various parts of the brain have to build infrastructure to one another in order to communicate and send signals, and this is where the real magic happens. By learning a new movement style, you've connected and expanded different networks of the brain, and by doing so, you allow the brain to become more efficient by being able to associate to other things.

Thus, the movements you learn in dance help you with the forms of karate, the forms of karate help you with the flow of a yoga sequence, and the postures of yoga help you learn how to ride a surf board. This goes beyond the mere physical.

Learning music, for example, has been shown to strengthen the parietal lobe, the same region of the brain involved in processing mathematical equations. If you're having problems in math class, perhaps learning the guitar or piano is your ticket to mathematical fluency.

The moral of the story? Diversify. The better equipped your brain is with learning new forms of movement, the easier a time you will have learning <u>anything.</u>

All life is energy. How efficiently energy is moved is what denotes good health from bad. Even as we strive to improve our movement routines, we can still shoot ourselves in the foot by eating the wrong food.

Nutrition

Let Thy Food be Thy Medicine

Of all the incredible technology human beings have created in the last few millennia, we have never come close to that which we individually call home. If you're fascinated by machines, then the human body won't fail to impress you. Our bodies embody the highest level of mechanics, electronics, and the most sophisticated circuitry in the world.

It took millions of years of evolution for us to become human, and yet within just a few hours, your system can take an apple, an orange, a piece of meat, and make it a part of *you*. Humans have never created a piece of machinery that can do this, and chances are, at least in my lifetime, we never will.

Your body, then, despite any level training and exercise you might have, is but the accumulation of food you have taken in. You are, therefore, what you eat. So the question is, "What are you?" Are you a crumbling body of fast food, bon bons, and

Cocoa Pebbles? Or is your body a temple, making it possible to experience life on deeper levels?

Food can be medicine, or it can be poison. Within each morsel of whole food, there are nutrients being harvested by your body. A body that has enough of what it needs in store has what is required to heal. A body that doesn't breaks down and dies, but not before enduring a huge amount of unnecessary suffering in the process.

If you're looking for a book that will give you a specific diet, you won't find it here. Given our diversity as a species, such a thing just doesn't exist. This chapter will center more on attitudes towards food, as well as what *not* to eat.

A Unique Breed

The conversation surrounding diet is complicated, to say the least. Hundreds of books and thousands of science-backed papers have been published on the subject, each heralding a different dietary lifestyle. There's the Paleo movement, then there's Keto and intermittent fasting, vegan, carnivore, Atkins, Mediterranean, and so the litany rolls into infinity. Spend an hour studying the various diets out there and your head will spin. All of these lifestyles are great, and they stand the test of time because they work for many people. Overall, however, they fail to address the root of the conversation concerning nutrition.

Humans have lived in a very diverse array of environments throughout the globe, and as it pertains to our capability for movement, this has been beneficial to us. However, from a dietary point of view, it draws some immediate problems. A quick survey of the animal kingdom, and you'll notice that animals rarely leave their niche environment. Unless catastrophe strikes, and the climate abruptly changes, most species will typically stay put in an environment that brings them food. The exception here would be for migratory species such as birds and bison. While it's true that many species migrate, these migration patterns suggest a cycle and tend to stay regular as the species move from one food source to another. In addition, these species tend to migrate to different locations that still yield similar environments.

Humans take it to the next level. Judging from the fossil records, we seem to have been a constantly roaming species throughout the last hundred thousand years. Starting in the great rift valley of East Africa, our ancestors spread north, eventually scattering - some going north into Europe, others turning east into Asia. From there, they crossed the land bridge between Siberia and Alaska to arrive in the Americas, eventually carving a path to what is now modern-day Chile. A quick glance at the map shows that just to walk that path directly would be over twenty-five thousand miles of footing it. Then consider the meandering path our ancestors took, exploring and settling into the mountains, valleys, and forests before necessity drove them onward to the next horizon. Twenty-five thousand miles doesn't come close to telling the story of how our globe-trotting ancestors colonized the earth.

Each new environment came with different challenges in the forms of pathogens and sources of food. Along the way, our genes were constantly keeping track, considering how to best adapt and meet the demands. As we settled into each new environment, our genes changed, and so did our physiology in order to reflect the environment around it.

Our expansion as a species then explains the complexity in regards to any conversation on diet. Consider the other subjects of this book: nature, movement, tribe, and sex. Regardless of the environment you're living in, not a lot changes in regards to these different folds of the human experience. Whether you live upon the African savanna, upon the windswept ice of the Arctic, or the basin of the Amazon River, you still live in a natural environment, characterized by the sights, sounds, and smells of nature. You're required to move every day in order to search for food and resources. You are a part of an intimate tribe of closely inter-dependent relationships, and you more than likely have a healthy sex life, considering the nearly universal attitude towards liberalism in this regard among foraging tribes. These parts of human life are therefore independent of environment. It matters little where you are.

Now we arrive at nutrition, and everything becomes *directly dependent upon your environment. Where you are* becomes *what is available* to eat, and what is available to eat becomes in turn *what you are.* If you're living in Africa, you're probably subsisting on a diet of antelope meat, fibrous vegetables, roots, and fruits. In the Arctic, you're subsisting off of a high-fat diet of seal meat. In the Amazon, you're eating acai berries, fruits, and mixed nuts. Therein lies the problem of nutrition. There is not, nor has there ever been, a universal diet for all of mankind. There are only dietary principles for specific lifestyles and body types.

The Human Diet(s), Written in Blood

Unless you donate blood or have needed a transfusion in the past, your blood type has probably seemed irrelevant in the grand scheme of things. Mainstream science on the subject can seem quite complex and as a result, the information available has gone largely unnoticed. Bad idea. Your blood type sets the ground work for both your immune and digestive systems, and without a proper understanding of it, you have a better chance of hitting a bullseye blind while throwing darts than you do of stumbling upon a healthy relationship with food.

Your blood-type dictates what type of antibodies your immune system will craft, and therefore what type of foreign antigens your system will attack. When a foreign body enters the system, immune antibodies launch an attack, clumping them together with sticky molecules called lectins. This is an immune system running effectively. By clumping the threats together, or agglutinating them, it is therefore easier to identify the criminals and shuttle them out of the body before they can cause harm.

All foods have antigens in the form of lectins. Different foods have different lectins, and this is where the problems arise. While lectins are useful in the body for agglutinating foreign bodies together, too much of a good thing can be very bad.

The body understands this, and as a result, ninety-five percent of lectins are removed from foods and shuttled out of the system. The remaining five percent, however, can cause problems. If for example you have an O blood type, but you consume high amounts of food with B-type lectins, the result is agglutination of the blood and inflammation throughout the blood stream. Another man's nourishment, indeed, is another man's poison.

Look on a pie chart of the globe, and you'll see four main blood types. Forty-three percent of people are O, thirty-two percent are A, fifteen percent are B, and the mere five percent remaining are AB. The story of blood type, like all parts of life, can be traced back throughout our evolutionary past. To this day, type O accounts for almost half of human beings on the planet, and that's where our story starts.

The Road from O to AB

Thomas Hobbes was wrong when he characterized the life of early humans as "nasty, brutish, and short." This didn't mean, however, that life was without work for early humans. Life was a daily challenge for Homo sapiens. Our ancestors worked hard for their survival, and much of that work went into finding food and braving the dangers of our Paleolithic world. Your average hunter-gatherer needed a robust immune system to fend off the cold as well as parasites in the environment, and they needed to be able to digest the simple and crude hand-to-mouth diet that they were often presented with. A bad piece of meat could kill you, and infection could mean losing a limb.

For these reasons, hunter-gatherer tribes will exhibit a predominant expression of O blood type. We spent more than ninety-five percent of our evolutionary history living as hunter-gatherers, and furthermore, this was the lifestyle our ancestors lived as they spread across the globe, thus seeding the planet with a predominant O expression.

With the development of agriculture came a new lifestyle in regards to both movement and food, and our genes had to adapt. As settlements grew, the first agrarian societies started to make their appearance on the world stage. Humans in the Middle East and Europe started cultivating the earth and living in more densely-packed communities where diseases tended to linger. Settlements became villages, and villages became cities. The life of the average person became more sedentary.

Cities drew a diverse array of people together and quickly become a sort of cultural and ethnic melting pot. Cities are therefore hot beds for diseases and as a result, blood type A was introduced. People with blood type A have a very tolerant immune system, as well as a particular resistance to the allergens present in agricultural foods, thus making them prime candidates for a primarily vegetarian lifestyle.

Survival of fittest within crowded society is the mark of blood type A, and you will surely see a predominance of the blood type in places with a long history of urbanized culture, such as western Europe.

While agrarian farming societies were flourishing in the western half of the Eurasian land-mass, a different experiment was unfolding upon the plains of Asia. People were living in nomadic herdsmen societies, where many people subsisted on the meats of herd animals, fermented dairy, and a diverse array of vegetables. Today, type B blood shows a predominance in east Asia where it originated, the Indian subcontinent, as well as northern Asia.

AB, the last blood type, seems to be an evolutionary hybrid of the first three blood types, and this is simply a testament to the increase in travel in the last couple hundred years. The last two hundred years have seen a marked increase in long-distance travel, and with this comes the coupling of different humans from far off places. AB could very well be nature's way of fusing the best traits from the blood types.

The vast majority of our evolution was accompanied by a very diverse array of foods. While this changed gradually over the last ten thousand years as societies developed, this gradual change is nothing to the abrupt change in the last one hundred years.

From the Apple to the PopTart: The Road to Food-Processing

When we talk of food processing, we typically imagine conveyor belts and assembly-line systems. The first processes for cleaning and storing food started many millennia ago around the cooking fires of our Paleolithic ancestors with the discovery of fire.

It's difficult to say an exact period when humans began to actively make and harness the energy of your typical camp fire. Regardless, it was a new threshold of possibility, allowing our ancestors to keep warm at night, ward off predators, and perhaps the most important in regards to the story of nutrition: cooking.

Prior to the development of cooking, our hominid ancestors spent several hours every day chewing the raw food available to us. By cooking our food, we softened it, allowing us to conserve crucial calories from chewing, as well as break the food down much more easily in our digestive systems. Over time, the bones in our jaws became less developed, allowing for our brains to expand. Cooking, perhaps, allowed us to become human.

Primitive methods of food storage followed, such as smoking, salting, and drying. This allowed humans to store more calories over the long-haul, ensuring better chances of survival when the seasons turned. It didn't matter if the bison hunt was a failure as long as food was stored for the winter.

From prehistoric societies to ancient and modern, these techniques for food preservation gradually spread, gaining contributions from ancient Greece, China, Peru, and European societies. As societies grew, they tended to grind against others, and this sparked conflict. The real developments in food preservation came with the needs of war.

"When the soldiers stand leaning on their spears, they are faint from want of food."

-Sun Tzu

War is the Father of All

Many of the things we take for granted are the products of war and imperial expansion. Back then, simply getting food to the battlefield was the nightmare of every commander. "An army marches upon its stomach," lamented the ambitious but fatigued Napoleon. His subsequent invasion of Moscow was almost entirely motivated by his need to take food stores. Fighting men need to eat. Twenty years prior in 1795, the French army offered twelve thousand francs to the first person who could develop a new and more efficient way of preserving food. Fifteen years later, Nicolas Appert presented his new canning method, thus allowing food stores to travel far and wide to support voyagers and soldiers.

The method wasn't widely adopted until much later, however. As late as the Crimean War period (1853-1856), the number one cause of soldiers dying in the field was not of being killed by the enemy, but by dying of scurvy. In other words, soldiers were dropping from nutrient deficiency. The same was true of life at sea. Sailors were routinely dying of malnutrition aboard ships. Many of the tales of *Flying Dutchman* ghost ships are thought to be attributed to entire crews dying from malnutrition. Appert's canning method wouldn't become popularized until the age of modern warfare

In 1941, the Japanese attacked Pearl Harbor, pulling the United States into the violent struggle of World War II. In response the United States transformed its industry into the most daunting war machine known to man. World War I had already popularized the method of canning, but now the government needed a way to get weapons and food to soldiers on two separate fronts: one in Europe fighting the Germans, and the other in the Pacific fighting the Japanese. To achieve this, the idea of non-perishable foods were explored.

Companies like the Hormel Meat Company had already been experimenting with these ideas. In 1937, they introduced canned pork and ham product, known as SPAM. By the end of the second World War, the U.S. military bought one hundred and fifty million pounds of Spam. In addition, the war effort brought on a wave of non-perishable products, such as M&Ms and Tootsie Rolls. Even instant coffee has its origins in military expedition.

At the end of the war, soldiers who had been in the field still craved these products, opening up the market for fast-food companies to fill the void. At the same time, the working middle-class was expanding and these workers often needed no-hassle, ready-to-eat meals, thus creating a booming opportunity for these companies to expand beyond their military endeavors. Thus, we can see how and why the American diet changed during the course of the twentieth century.

In the United States, the war-time food distribution system never stopped. We simply kept going, thinking that greater yields of "food" meant more well-fed people. The problem is that these foods consist primarily of empty calories and were never meant to be eaten for the long-term. They were meant to temporarily energize soldiers in the field, not to nourish an entire society for years. While the war-time food system began with good intentions, the situation that is has led to can't be defended.

The Birth of Food Engineering

The obvious question is, "Why eat food that kills you?" The dark truth is that many of don't have a choice. The food that we've become addicted to has been slowly engineered over the last five decades in order to be as addicting as possible. Meanwhile, most people live in urbanized environments, and fewer and fewer people nowadays have access to whole-food markets right around the corner. But how did we get here? The story of food engineering starts in the 1970s with a man named Howard Moskowitz.

Moskowitz discovered that when the perfect combination of fat, salt, and sugar were present in foods, the pleasure experience of eating was optimized. Pleasure, in this case, is derived by a neurotransmitter called dopamine. When you eat something sweet, your brain responds by giving you a dopamine hit, and this is what makes you feel that nice brain buzz when you bite into a candy bar. As your brain becomes accustomed to the dopamine rush, it responds by making more dopamine receptors, requiring more dopamine for the same hit, thus making fertile ground for addiction.

After his discovery, Moskowitz was sought out by all the big-name food companies who could afford his advice on what he described as the "bliss point." It didn't stop there with the perfect combination of fat, salt, and sugar. Food became crunchier, fiber was removed allowing it to slide down the throat, and nutrients were removed, thus making you eat more to become sated.

Your typical fast-food sandwich or taco is but a combination of all these developments, and this is to say nothing for the myriad of commercially baked goods and candy out on the market. These foods are all loaded with sugar, fat, and salt in the perfect combination, and they have virtually no nutritional value.

The companies responsible for manufacturing these foods aren't thinking of your health. They are thinking about profits, and unbeknownst to the masses, they've been paying billions annually to research and engineer the most addictive foods possible to keep you hooked. It's a win-win for the companies engineering these foods. Because they are addictive and lacking in nutritional value, you continue to buy and eat more and more of them. This is due to a part deeply embedded within your brain called the hypothalamus. The hypothalamus regulates satiety by keeping track of nutrient needs within the body. When the brain senses a deficiency in nutrients, it signals the body to become hungry and look for food that can supply those nutrients. In a perfect world, you could find some fruit, nuts, and seeds, and maybe some meat that would supply all the nutrients, and the hypothalamus, like a worker checking nutritional boxes on a clip board, would signal the body to relax and digest.

Because the food lacks nutrients, the hypothalamus continues to signal the body to remain hungry. This explains why people can't stop eating. It also explains the nutrient deficiencies that are wide-spread throughout America despite having plenty of food. We lack many nutrients such as fiber and iron to omega-3 amino acids. You keep pounding the food in, and you become hungrier and hungrier. Imagine it. In the most well-fed country on the planet, people are dying of malnutrition. We have more food than we can possibly eat, but it's not worth shit. In reality, what is typically on the American dinner plate is not food.

It's a Drug

Look at the label on any commercially-made product you'll see one common ingredient: sugar. Here's a fact: the average Westerner consumes more sugar during breakfast than your average hunter-gatherer would during a month in the bush. The bulk of our evolution as humans was spent living in a slightly ketogenic state where our bodies were deprived of sugar. Sure, you'd find a bushel of apples on a good day and gorge yourself, but these instances were more the exception than the rule.

Meanwhile, a "healthy" breakfast in the modern world of orange juice, oatmeal, and yogurt yields almost fifty grams of sugar. This is to say nothing for the bread many people eat for lunch, as well as the rice and pasta that is present at many dinner tables as a staple food. All in all, most human beings in a single day get well over one hundred grams of sugar, and this is assuming you're not drinking soda and eating fast food. If you are, go ahead and triple the original number.

Sugar is the most addictive drug in the world. Similar to cocaine, it lights up pleasure centers of the brain immediately upon taste and promotes a surge of energy followed by an immediate crash. You usually need more sugar to keep going. This starts a vicious cycle of eating and re-eating until a person can hardly function without the stimulant.

You might ask yourself, "If something is poison, how can you be allowed to sell it?" It's a good question. The answer to it is this: in liberal, free-market cultures such as the United States, you're allowed to sell it *because* it sells well. The consumer wants it, and people buy it. Therefore, you keep manufacturing the product, and people get more and more addicted to it. Cigarettes, hard alcohol, fast food sandwiches, soda pop, unnecessary household cleaning products, etc. You're talking about poison when you mention any one of these products. But consumers want them, and in a liberal society, the consumer is king.

It's not like there's little shame in selling these products. The general population is at least somewhat aware that they are ingesting poison. It's for this reason that sugar-toting companies like Coca-Cola spend billions annually in order to shift attention from their product. In 2007, the company launched their "Exercise is Medicine" campaign in order to sway the medical establishment to use level of activity as a vital sign, and to prescribe physical exercise as a treatment for sickness. "It's not the massive payload of sugar crammed into every can that's giving you diabetes and heart disease," says the company. "You're just not moving enough." What's so sinister about this dangerous notion is that it's partly true. The average human being in the modern world doesn't move enough. But by pushing this notion, you solve one half of the problem while providing a smoke screen for the other. "It's not our soda that's killing you. Crack open a bottle, go for a run, and then quench your thirst with another." And yet, physiology doesn't lie.

When you consume sugar, insulin is released into the system, signaling cells to open up to shuttle the sugar out of the blood stream. When the cells become full, more insulin is released to pack the sugar into the already bulging cells. Once it doesn't work, sugar stays in the bloodstream, and you have diabetes. Long-term diabetes leaves organs and blood vessels damaged, eventually ending in death. The problem isn't insulin resistance. It's sugar. Stop eating sugar, and your baseline insulin will lower. If you are a Type 2 diabetic, quitting sugar will have countless benefits to your condition. It's that simple, and yet you'll never hear it from the big-name brands that sell sugar to the masses.

The bottom line is this: these companies do not care about your health, only the bottom line of their yearly revenue. They will sell you poison, watch smugly while you die a slow and painful death, and then they'll proceed to do the same to your family and friends. These are wolves; as criminal as any of the countless thieves or murderers that society can produce.

Think of that the next time you indulge in that sugary cereal, that pastry cake, or that fizzy soda. You're nothing but a number to these people, and you're being sacrificed at the altar of their prosperity.

What a Human Should Eat: A Discussion

To start off, every person must view themselves as the recipient of a very diverse evolutionary heritage. You are an individual, and you must experiment with your own body. Try a food out for a day or two. If it gives you energy, it's good for you. If you feel tired and lethargic, say goodbye to it.

Know your blood type. Depending on your blood type, certain foods will immediately be rendered suspect by your immune system. If this happens, your body will become a battleground, causing energy-fatigue and inflammation, both of which will sap your overall vitality.

Lifestyle and aspiration is also a factor that must be considered. Your body is literally the accumulation of the food that you take in. You must ask yourself, then, what kind of body you would like. Do you want a body that can lift a house? What about a body that can sit and meditate? Are you an Olympic athlete or are you an academic who needs to process vast amounts of information every day? Every scenario involves a different ideal eating lifestyle. While there is no single diet that is ideal for everyone, there are a few rules that can guide you.

Go Ketosis

The keto lifestyle has become popular for a reason. There wasn't a lot of sugar in the world of our hunter-gatherer ancestors. Take a walk into the mountains and woods and you'll see that the bulk of food available to you will have a lot of fiber and fat, but not a lot of sugar. The vast majority of the hunter-gatherer world was subsisting off of food such as this, and as a result, they were in a slightly ketogenic state.

For this reason, the keto lifestyle seems to be the closest thing we have to an optimal eating-lifestyle for most human beings, especially first thing in the morning when the body is high in cortisol. Cortisol is a stress hormone that makes you feel alert. Back in the day, this was important for our ancestors, because it meant we could keep vigilant on the lookout for dangers in the environment as we searched for food.. It also has the added benefit of signaling the body to burn fat, thus making your body a fat burning machine at this time of the day.

Meanwhile, the average human being gets more sugar for breakfast than a hunter-gatherer would find in a month living in the bush. By eating sugar of any kind first thing in the morning, you are going directly against the rhythm of your body, and you're planting the seeds for cravings for later in the day.

Foods like avocado, nuts and seeds, coconut and olive oils, and eggs (if you're not vegan) can be very beneficial to your system. By eating this way, you'll feel much more energized throughout the day, and your brain and body will be much happier.

Go Whole

Real food doesn't have a label, nor is it packaged neatly in colorful plastic wrapping. The closer you can find food to the source, the better, in many more ways that just your health.

Food is only a problem in the modern world because, in reality, it's not real food. We're eating bullshit calories that are designed to keep us hungry and malnourished. Our food is fake, plain, and simple. A good way to follow this rule is simply to shop on the perimeter of your market where you'll find the produce and to avoid the inside aisles where you'll find the packaged, sugary sweets.

Whole food is anything from apples and oranges, raw nuts and seeds, to vegetables like broccoli, kale, and carrots. Eat foods like these and watch the immediate effect they have your vitality and health. Bonus points if you shop local at a farmers' market.

Go Local

Why eat local? Not only is it better for your health, but it's also better for your community. When you buy an apple, for example, at your local supermarket, you're buying a piece of fruit that has been shipped to you from across the world by one of four major food companies. These food companies work through subsidiaries in a particular region and contract workers from that region to pick and package the produce before transporting through a vast system of transportation to its final destination. Efficient though it may be, the process has many glaring factors. The workers themselves usually aren't paid fairly, the process relies on pesticides and refrigeration to keep the produce fresh, and because you buy the food from these faceless companies, you make it much harder for your local farmer to survive. These large corporations then take your hard-earned money and use it to sway politics. The system is vast, and it is very impressive. Then again, so was the Third Reich. Few would claim upon examination that a system that ultimately degrades local farmers is a good thing, much like you'd rarely find a person that claims that Hitler was onto something with his final solution. By allowing these companies to take our money, we not only degrade our food and our health, but we allow resources to be sapped from our local communities.

When you go to the farmers' market, you allow money to stay local, and you can then pay your local farmers to continue to do what they do. Otherwise, you'll be left with a world of industrialized farms chugging out pesticide laden "produce," and you'll wonder why sickness is spreading like a plague.

And Sometimes, Go No Food at All

Let's talk fasting. The benefits for it are incredible, yet here in the West, fasting is often regarded as a dangerous practice. The idea of forgoing food for any length of time will set most Westerners sweating. Even those that fast regularly will often be regarded with suspicion. It's ironic that it would be this way in a culture founded upon Judeo-Christian ethics. What do you think Jesus was doing out in the desert for forty days? The guy was fasting.

It would require a separate book in order to communicate all the various benefits of forgoing food, but to answer the question "Why should you fast?", I'll focus on one benefit: healthier cells.

Your body is made up of hundreds of billions of cells, and the health of these cells collectively is what dictates your health.

When a cell dies, a new cell is immediately replicated to replace the dead cell. Eventually, the rate between dying/replicating increases, and when cells are dying at a faster rate than being replaced, the body begins to age. This is old news.

Interesting things start to happen once we stop eating. The first is this: insulin levels begin to lower. Your body releases insulin as a means of signaling the body to store energy. First stop is the cells. Food is broken down into glycogen and then stored here. Once the cells are full, the body needs a back-up plan for preventing the sugar from staying in the bloodstream. It does this by converting the sugars and storing them as fat. The problem is that if the body is always storing energy, it's never getting rid of its' excess (like fat or cancerous cells, for example) When insulin levels drop, the body can then shift out of "energy storage," and into "energy burning." This is how fasting works - by using the energy that's already stored in the body as fuel while new energy isn't coming in to be processed. But this is only the beginning.

Aside from fat-burning, lowered insulin levels allow the body to organize itself more efficiently. Two processes are responsible for this: autophagy and apoptosis. This is where things get really cool. When cells are deprived of outside energy, they begin utilizing their own. Membranes are created with the purpose of eating up the excess parts of the cell which aren't needed, thereby allowing it to run more efficiently. This is the cellular level equivalent of a serial hoarder finally cleaning their house after years of "acquiring" new things. Autophagy is the process that your body uses to literally clean itself at the cellular level.

Some cells are too far gone ,however, and some are even malign and working against the body. Think cancer cells. For these cells, autophagy isn't enough. Killer T cells are produced and then travel throughout the body signaling these dying cells to self-destruct. In this way, through fasting, the body becomes healthier.

Even with the above rules, each person must be treated as an individual in what they eat and how they eat their food. Circling back to the earlier discussion on blood types, depending on the type of blood you have, your immune system will create certain antibodies. Antibodies attack certain lectins, and there are a wide variety of lectins that exist in food. If you eat a food that has lectins contrary to your immune system, your immune system will mount an attack upon the foreign lectins. If you're eating a lot of this food, even if it is a "healthy food," your blood will agglutinate, causing inflammation and eventually damage to tissues and organs.

Have an understanding of your blood type, and find the foods that are good for you. Above all, experiment with your own body. Try a food out for a few days. If it agrees with you, you will feel energy from eating it. If not, you'll feel lazy and lethargic. Every human being has an individual gene make-up with different preferences in food. Get to know your own, and don't let some "food guru" tell you that there is one way of eating for everybody.

Part III

Community

Tribe

Eons ago in an era that vastly predates the human species, the first life appeared upon Earth in the form of prokaryotes. These were very simple, single-celled organisms that swam around in search of energy that could sustain them. These first prokaryotic cells eventually banded together to form the first eukaryote. One eukaryotic cell is formed by thousands of single-celled prokaryotes. A single organ of the human body is made up of hundreds of billions of eukaryotic cells, all collaborating in unison so that the organ can function. The human body, then, comprised of many different organs and tissues, is a nearly unfathomable conglomeration of cellular cohesion, all working in unison so that the entire unit may function. Just as the individual cell is more likely to survive working in unison with others, humans are much more likely to survive in groups. Our ability to exist together and cooperate at large-scale is why we were able to dominate every environment we set foot in. One scrawny human being can't do much against an African lion. Dozens of humans together can slaughter entire prides, and even drive the species to extinction.

Agrarian society changed how we socialize, but that change didn't happen overnight. The road from small hunter-gatherer bands to globalized society is one that stretches back over ten thousand years, and it can be seen as a progression of installments. With each new installment, the community grew, new problems emerged, and the system itself had to expand and become more sophisticated in order to control the increasingly diversified population. As the system grew, however, the links between each person became less pronounced. Fast forward to modern day, where a person can spend an entire day without even seeing another human being, and you begin to see a problem.

Having systematically gamed every pursuit of survival into our distribution systems, it is no longer obvious that we humans need each other. While our nervous systems need close relations with other human beings, humans themselves don't require one another for life in the modern world. And yet, as we drift further and further apart, separated by the institutions of modern society, we find that our paths become distorted and unclear. We no longer know how to live, or what to live for.

The Deepest of Questions

Take a moment and think. What would you die for? I'll be impressed if you can name anything without second guessing yourself. It's a difficult question specifically because it is far too broad. The idea of setting such high evolutionary stakes upon any one thing besieges the mind with angst. If, however, you asked "*Who* would you die for?", it becomes suddenly clear for most people, and this is significant.

Who to die for has been, throughout human history, the deepest question people have been called to ask of themselves.

The ability itself to ask and contemplate this question in the first place is what separates humans from other members of the animal kingdom. Whole religious paradigms have been founded upon such questions for a reason. Who or what you'll die for will dictate how you will live. And how you live will decide the nature of how and maybe who you will die for.

Every creature on the planet yearns to live, and every creature will fight like hell in the face of an existential threat. Self-preservation is paramount throughout the majority of the animal kingdom, and yet it's not necessarily so with mammals. We all tear up at the thought of a she-bear or lioness throwing her life away for her cubs. We immortalize tales of soldiers dying on the battlefield to save others within their unit, and the most popular of tales ever told are of people willfully going to a torturous death for the sake of others.

One popular story is that of the three hundred Spartans. In 480 B.C, three thousand Greeks stood within the pass of Thermopylae. Theirs was a suicide mission: to hold the pass against an invading Persian army that commanded over one hundred thousand troops. Vastly outmanned, the allies held the pass for over four days until they were slaughtered to the last man. The Spartan King Leonidas was beheaded and crucified as a symbol of the Persian king's distaste. The mere tale of this exploit caused the rest of the Greek city-states (hitherto hellbent on exterminating one another) to unite, and the following spring upon the plains of Plateau, the Persian army stood across from an army of fifty thousand free Greeks, all fighting in defense of their homelands. The Greeks were, again, vastly outnumbered; but fueled by the tale of sacrifice, they utterly routed the Persians.

The mother of all stories of self-sacrifice, at least as to how it pertains to Western culture is that of Jesus. The son of a Jewish carpenter, Jesus spent much of his life as a roaming ascetic who spurned niceties in the service of his people. Jesus traveled by foot up and down the Israeli countryside, preaching the good news of salvation and deliverance from beneath the Roman heel. This was all well and good until he flew directly in the face of many Jewish authorities of the day. We don't know much about the life of Jesus, but we know this: the man willfully walked to his death, one in which he was brutally beaten and humiliated before being nailed to a Roman cross.

Whether you're talking about Jesus, Ghandi, William Wallace, or the three hundred Spartans, all of the tales have a common thread. And they spread like wildfire among human beings for a reason.

A Darker Question

If what to die for is to portray a more noble bearing in human beings, what about our darker side? Indeed, what to kill for might be a far more relevant question to ask. And humans have proven to incredibly good at killing throughout history, especially if it's in the name of something they believe in.

In regards to the question, we often scoff at the behavior of other human beings throughout history. How, for example, could people like you and I have participated in Nazi Germany? Why do millennials run off and join a group like ISIS, a group that, along with the many atrocities committed, simply has no coherent worldview? How could the Imperial Japanese soldiers have acted so monstrously towards the citizens of Nanking, and how could scientists of the same Imperial regime conduct such harrowing scientific experiments upon Chinese prisoners? Why is every major rock band, from Motley Crue to the Red Hot Chili Peppers, followed around by legions of groupies who will utterly degrade themselves sexually for inclusion?

The answer to all of these questions can be found between our ears. The human brain is the most complicated known technology in the universe, but one thing has grown increasingly clear: the human brain is a social brain.

Humans are Mammals

The sociality of human beings can be traced back two hundred and fifty million years to the first mammal. This can hardly be overstated. Dinosaurs were still strutting around during this stage of the game, and they would have another two hundred million years of dominance before a meteor presumably crashed into the Yucatan Peninsula.

Long before there were any primates, mammals diverged from the tree of life in nature's latest experiment. The mammalian brain was different in that it came with an upgrade. The reptilian brain consists of the brain stem, cerebellum, and hypothalamus. These parts of the brain control basic motor function, satiety, and primal instinct. Mammals are equipped with the reptile brain and more.

Along with the reptile brain, all mammals have a limbic brain, and this is where things get interesting. Among other parts, what sets mammals apart from others animals is in a part of the limbic brain called the anterior cingulate cortex (ACC). This particular part of new neural circuitry allows mammals to feel social pain, and this is an important distinction. That pain you feel when you are picked last for a game, when you're dumped by a lover, or suffer public humiliation is all facilitated by this part of the brain and is uniquely mammalian. It's hard to overstate the significance here: a crocodile doesn't bat one prehistoric eyelash at what other crocs think. She is a solitary creature. She'll even eat her own offspring if times are tough. Mammals, in contrast, survive *through* group cohesion. They take care of one another, even die for one another, and we have the ACC to thank for this.

The important finding here is that social pain is in fact real pain. When someone tells you they have a broken heart, you know that they are speaking metaphorically. They are not literally bleeding on the inside. Yet the pain they are feeling lights up the exact same part of the brain as would a broken bone or a torn rotator cuff. Why would evolution program us in such a seemingly counterproductive way? Physical pain is bad enough, and as most people know firsthand, a broken heart will often make you *want* to die.

This social pain that we feel spurs us to assist one another. When a baby is separated from its mother, the ACC will light up, causing it to feel the pain of that separation and vocalize the pain it is feeling. A mother, on the other side, will feel the same pain, and rush to the child's aid. The crying of an infant is one of the most easily identified sounds in human beings, and for a very good reason. Children are defenseless. We all recognize this, which is why we rush to provide aid. Social pain is a defining characteristic among most mammals. Then come the primates, who build even more upon the social brain.

Primates take things up a notch, being endowed with a neo-cortex built upon the mammalian brain. This is the large, bulky part of the brain that we typically think of in humans and is, in fact, the very part which allows us to store and process such a vast amount of information. When you learn anything new, the information is stored temporarily in the hippocampus, which acts as a sort of temporary center of storage. While you sleep at night, the new information is then processed to the neo-cortex, which acts as a more permanent center of storage.

A neo-cortex means that the organism can store more information about the surrounding environment, skills relatable to survival, and, you guessed it, relationships. The NC allows primates to identify not only what other members of the pack are doing, but also *what they're looking at*, thus allowing the animal to make an inference upon what the other is thinking. The upgrade means an ability to keep track of a much more dynamic social network. Chimpanzees know not only who they have feuds with, but who other members of their troupe are feuding with. Such awareness of the group allowed primates to live among more and more members within a single group.

Bonobos and chimpanzees (our closest relatives on the evolutionary tree) both can live within groups of up to one hundred and fifty members. Do the math, and this means that each member has to have a working memory and awareness of thousands of potential relationships among the group. Which members are having sex, what feuds exist and between who, who is showing signs of breaking apart from the troupe altogether. It all matters. With so many members and relationships to keep track of, the neo-cortex becomes an indispensable part of the brains arsenal.

Both of the above developments with the mammalian capability in cognition allowed for unprecedented communal cooperation, but they also came with a negative consequence. The new capabilities that allow mammals to live communally also come with the caveat that our wellbeing is literally tied to our relationships with others. Intimacy and social belonging reflects a state of neuro-chemistry. As we'll soon see, loneliness reflect its own.

As humans, we are wired for community. Our neuro-circuitry evolved over millions of years to reward us for community-pro actions, as well as keep track of our place within the hierarchy of that community. The neuro-dynamic between serotonin and octopamine levels are but a reflection of how we feel in stature within a group. A high ratio of serotonin/octopamine produces confidence, while the opposite produces a feeling of inferiority. The leader of any group will always reflect a high serotonin level.

Humans may be communal specifically because of our physical frailty as a species. Assailed on all sides by a dangerous and primordial world, humans found security and strength amongst one another. The world outside can be full of danger and chaos, but so long as you are among the tribe, you are safe within the warm light of the campfire.

All of this means that we are biologically biased towards recognizing and responding positively to symbols of community regardless of how those symbols manifest. Whether the group has insidious intent is irrelevant as far as your brain is concerned. Adolf Hitler wanted to watch the world burn. That didn't stop millions of zealots from jumping on the gravy train. "It's better to be inside a bad group and alive," says the mammal brain, "than to be out and alone in the cold," and it's for this reason that humans will follow a good leader, even if that leader has a monstrous vision.

For the above reasons, we recognize sports teams and rock bands because they represent a genuine symbol of community among the members, as well as the art and performance that become possible when human beings live and strive to create *together*. Likewise, we identify strongly with our favorite TV shows like *The Office* and *Friends* because they emphasize the efforts and struggle within an evolving community. Strip away the group dynamic, and you'd have TV productions that would crash and burn within a season. A paper company in Scranton? Everyday life in New York City? Excuse me while I yawn.

But wait: *living through life and love, navigating heartbreak and disappointment, and finding a deeper understanding of life supported by your best pals - that's* Friends. *The antics and hijinks that make daily office life bearable, the relationships that grow over time between co-workers, all seen through the lens of a hapless boss and the often exasperated people that work beneath him. That's* The Office.

Life is hard and times get tough, says the theme of both TV series. *But together, we'll get through it, no matter what.* And look at the result: both TV series, as mundane as they may be, are world-wide phenomena that transcend cultural, ethnic, and even religious boundaries. We recognize and even crave their narratives because they tap into a deeply primordial part of our brains. It is that part of us that this chapter will seek to explore.

Maslow was Wrong

Basic physiological needs are typically understood through the lens of the Maslow pyramid. An American psychologist in the twentieth century, Abraham Maslow ranked the needs of human beings through five levels. Physiological needs such as food, water, and shelter came first. Next were secondaries such as health, property, and employment. Only after these do we approach the third level of the pyramid: love, friendship, community, and belonging. Because Maslow was looking at the needs of humans within society, he missed one crucial point.

Humans are primates, primates are mammals, and all mammals are born immature, vulnerable and dependent upon their parents for their survival. If you are human, you are reading this book only because you survived your childhood. And this was possible only because someone (presumably your parents) felt so deeply attuned and connected to your needs that whenever they heard you cry, they were compelled to come to your aid.

Your need for food is irrelevant if you have no means for getting to it. Sociality, then, among human beings should be at the base of the pyramid. You'd have never survived the first year of your life without it, after all.

If expectation is the root of suffering, then what happens to a human brain that expects continuous social contact with others? For an idea of this, we can look at the most extreme example of social isolation. In the darkest corners of the penitentiary systems that span the globe, we can peer into how and what happens when you force a social animal to be isolated.

Solitary Apes

Ninety miles south of Denver, beneath the shadows of the Rocky Mountain chain, is the ADX High-Security Prison. The most notorious prison in the continental US, the complex boasts state of the art technology to keep prisoners within, while the very design of the prison itself seems to have perfected the art of solitary confinement.

Each prisoner spends twenty-three hours a day in a cell the size of a walk-in closet. Within this space, he eats, sleeps, showers, exercises, writes and reads, and goes to the bathroom. Food is delivered three times a day through a metal slot. For one hour a day, he's given time in a concrete cage slightly larger than his cell for an opportunity to "exercise." His only contact with another human being is the guard who is trained to ignore him. He can't see the nearby mountains or sky, and soon perhaps, he won't even remember what the world outside looks like.

Institutionalized solitary confinement began in 1829 at the Eastern Penitentiary of Philadelphia. Based on religious ideals among the Quakers, it was believed that if locked in a stone room with nothing but a Bible, a person would repent of their sinful human nature and, free from the evils of the modern world, would finally return to God. A noble idea, as well as an experiment, in theory. However, it's yet another example of what happens when religious institutions fail to understand human nature.

By the 1830s, it was clear that solitary confinement was a failure. The evidence became unmistakable that the noble experiment was causing massive psychiatric damage to its inmates, leading to psychiatric and physical breakdown. Many died during confinement due to the resulting delirium, self-harm, and suicide. For the lucky few that made it out, they found themselves confronted by an alien world, filled with an unbearable sense of social anxiety.

It's important to remember that choice in the matter plays a large role. If I decide to go out into the woods alone for a week, that's called solitude. Every religious figure from Jesus to Muhammad sought solitude in this form. But they *chose* to do so. If, however, you lock me in a box away from people, the neuro-chemistry will reflect quite differently.

In the 1950s studies were done on the effects of solitary confinement in order to show these cerebral changes. Using baby Rhesus monkeys, Dr. Harry Harlow conducted an experiment to see what would happen if you took socialized monkeys who had grown up among a group and forced them to be alone. In a particularly haunting experiment, he separated groups of monkeys and put them into separate cages, and he waited. It didn't take long to produce an effect. After a few weeks of total isolation, the monkeys began exhibiting disturbing signs. They would cower in their cages, rock back and forth manically, and occasionally would scream in endless succession. The most disturbing, however, was what happened when the monkeys were placed back together *after* the same period of time.

Apart from one another, on opposite sides of the cages, the monkeys would huddle, clearly unable to cope with the sudden social event. The experiment would eventually end in violence. Unable to cope with the situation, the monkeys would viciously attack one another until they were separated.

Solitary confinement as a practice was largely abandoned from institutional correctional facilities in the nineteenth century, only to resurface a century later in the 1980s when growing populations, not to mention the growing strife within society, caused more and more people to be crammed into prisons.

In 1983, two prison guards at Marion Penitentiary were murdered by inmates on two separate incidents on the same day. The warden placed the entire prison on lockdown. Concerns for the safety of staff were revisited, and within a few years many other institutions around the country began following the lockdown guidelines. This all culminated in the construction of Pelican Bay in California, a massive institution where solitary confinement became the normal procedure for a growing and increasingly unpredictable population of inmates.

Because they are criminals, it's easy to dismiss the following studies, saying, "They made their decisions. Let them rot." As we'll see, not only is this simply naive and inhumane, but it will no doubt have an awful backlash on society.

The effects of such a practice are clear in the literature - that solitary confinement breaks down the parts of the brain that allow us to be socially adept, making people more unpredictable and therefore more dangerous, further compounding and exacerbating the situation at hand. You might as well put a house fire out by throwing more wood upon the flame.

As technology has improved throughout the centuries, we've been able to peer into the human brain in ways that we never could before. Having applied the technology to the human nervous system, we now know what happens as a result of prolonged social isolation.

In the Absence of the Unpredictable

Socializing is no easy affair, especially when you're surrounded by strangers. It requires the brain to make inferences and associations of people over time. Once you notice the patterns of another human being, they become more familiar, you feel safer, and you might even think of them as a friend. You trust them because you know their patterns. Socializing is, in effect, a form of exercise for the human brain.

Though the brain only accounts for two percent of the total body weight, its intermingled tissues require over twenty percent of the body's energy. A large part of the human brain is taken up by the vastly large neo-cortex which, as mentioned earlier, exists almost solely to understand people in a relational sense. Just like any muscle, it must be trained. When the neo-cortex degrades due to solitary confinement, the effect is disastrous.

Among inmates in solitary confinement, self-abuse is rampant. Inmates routinely cut themselves, bang their heads against the wall, and flood their toilets, simply for a sense of novelty. When they are finally let out among other people, their neo-cortex has often atrophied to the point of not understanding who the people around them are. The newly-created anxiety often leads them to violence, thus creating a vicious cycle of solitary to communal living that can't be escaped.

Because many of these inmates that were exposed to this kind of disciplinary punishment will be out on the street in just a few months, this will inevitably become a scourge on society. If their ability to socialize deteriorates to the point of not being able to cope being near small groups, what will happen when these people are exposed to a shopping mall or standstill traffic? The writing is on the wall. We just have to heed its wisdom.

We need to ask ourselves if this is the path that is most effective. If we are subjecting real human beings to social isolation, a practice that has been shown time and time again to be toxic and impairing, are we not shooting ourselves in the foot later when these people inevitably relapse into conflict when they return to society?

Human beings shouldn't be subjected to forced isolation for the same reason that a dog should never be whipped, beaten, and starved. You reap what you sow. Should you fashion a beast, don't cry foul should it decide to rip your throat out.

The reality of the current situation is that with population increase and the coming surge of mentally unstable people, the use of solitary confinement will only have to continue to grow. Then where will we be?

With two hundred and fifty million years of cerebral development, we are essentially hard-wired for community. We can trace our roots back to the mammalian limbic system, followed by our primates cousins who come equipped with the neo-cortex. Finally, we arrive at the distinctly human brain.

One thousand apes together, of practically any kind, would be a disastrous affair, and yet somehow humans make it work. In fact, we're currently the only member of the ape family that can. The frontal lobe and the pre-frontal cortex that resides upon it give us the ability to not only live communally and strategically like our primate cousins, but also to *harmonize* together on a vast scale in ways that dwarf our ape cousins.

There's another word for this "harmonizing," as it is called in the literature. Since the dawn of agrarianism, we've called it society. With a better understanding of the social brain, let's take a walk through history and look at where we came from, where we are, and if we're not careful, where we will inevitably end up.

The March to Civilization

Homo sapiens is a very social species, but only at a very local level. Until agriculture, we lived in intimate hunter-gatherer groups that rarely numbered more than a few dozen people. In such a small group, every person is a member of an intimately woven and interconnected group dynamic where every person knows every other. Every moment of life is scrutinized by fellow peers, and there is rarely a moment of being truly alone. It's safe to say that virtually no human being living in modern society can expect such a dynamic. This is the same dynamic you could expect to find in today's deployed military units, and it is why war is often so intoxicating. It's not about the fighting, it's about the intimacy in your relationships.

In 2018, while still in the navy, I was deployed on the *USS Essex* for seven months. For over two hundred days, I was a member of a twenty-man group of helicopter mechanics that worked twelve-hour shifts in a space probably no bigger than your kitchen. At such a small-group level, there are no secrets: I knew who was having marital issues within the group, I knew who was sleeping with whom, I knew what conflicts existed and who they were between, and I knew generally every detail about that person's life.

Deployment often sucked, but that kind of group intimacy makes you understand what's important. I was increasingly aware over that seven months that if anybody messed with me, I'd have twenty people racing to have my back in an instant. There's a certain strength in knowing this, and an all-pervading weakness to the human condition at not knowing it. This is the kind of support that you can't always expect to receive among the masses.

As the population grows, humans will organize into different groups much like a growing company will organize itself into different departments, thus beginning to separate certain members from others. It can be said that the average tie of intimacy between group members severs over time as the population itself grows bigger, simply because there is less face time between members of the group. In addition, stockpiles of resources begin to become a reality, causing a need for administration.

Hunter-gatherer tribes are fiercely egalitarian specifically because there aren't many resources to go around. Among most hunter-gatherer tribes even today, selfishness is a cardinal sin. With so few resources, there's simply no room for hoarding because it would undoubtably spark jealousy in others. Cohesion means survival. An ounce of discord can threaten that cohesion and, therefore, the entire tribe. It makes little sense to hoard a tool or implement if everyone else is going to use it anyways. This extends to everything from tools and food, and especially to sex partners, but more on that in the next chapter.

Add to this the fact that the group is typically nomadic, moving with the season, and *not* having too many resources can become a necessity. If we live communally and have to carry everything on our backs, how many pots and pans do we actually need? This mode of thinking, however, becomes obsolete once a populace plants roots and becomes sedentary.

Resources accumulate, and once they accumulate they must be divided and allocated. Now that people have their own resources, each member becomes less inter-dependent upon the other members. For the first time, self-interest and personal property become a reality, further aiding the march of class distinctions.

Eventually multiple villages become inter-connected through trade, and kingdoms rise from the roots of these primitive tribes. At this point, as many as hundreds of thousands of humans are living beneath the same societal symbol. To govern such a vast number of people is a very difficult affair, and it begs the question - how do you cement people together who don't know one another? How do you trust another human being who you've only just met but nonetheless must do business with?

Why Humans are Different

Humans transformed from insignificant apes to rulers of the planet in a relatively short span of time. This is puzzling when you consider the few advantages we have over other animal species. There is no shortage of animals that can run faster, fight more ferociously, see farther and with more clarity, and detect fainter smells. And though we like to think so, we are not necessarily more intelligent when it comes to survival. Take a naked human being and a chimpanzee and drop them out in the forest with nothing but instinct and intelligence to survive, and my money will surely be on the chimpanzee. One on one, humans are simply no match for most other animals. One hundred humans, one thousand humans, however, against any other animal? We'll win every time.

The one definite advantage human beings have over other species is in our collective cohesion. We can socialize and cooperate with a large amount of other humans, and we can do so very flexibly. Other animals are social, yes, but they must choose between an ability for flexibility or working together in large-scale.

Wolves and lions can cooperate flexibly, but only in small groups. Cram a thousand lions into a subway train or ten thousand wolves into a stadium, and the result will be a bloodbath. Humans do this on a daily basis.

Bees and ants can live in colonies of thousands, but only in rigid, unchanging hierarchies. If the climate changes, or a beehive is invaded by killer hornets, the entire hive can't simply decide to orient itself differently against the threat. Yet again, we humans do this routinely, having the ability to change our societies almost overnight to defend against danger.

Humans are the only animal that can routinely congregate on a large scale and do so flexibly.

Your average military member will only meet less than a percentage of fellow service members, yet the army itself remains intact. Google employs over one hundred thousand people, the vast majority of whom will never meet one another. Yet Google thrives as a business. How can such a thing be possible? The answer is in the stories we tell.

Narratives: The Story-Telling Ape

We're the best story-tellers on the planet. Our ability to create stories means that we can imagine new futures and actively create those futures for the coming generation. As I'm sitting here at my computer, I'm living in the imagination of Steve Jobs, who spent his life visualizing how the Internet would reshape human life. Likewise, every time I sit in conversation with people of different color or ethnicity, I'm sitting in the imagination of Martin Luther King Jr., who imagined a world where his children would be judged by the content of their hearts and not the color of their skin. You and I are currently living in the imagined future of the many great people who came before us, from Ghandi and Mandela to the founding fathers. Our children, likewise, will be living in the futures that we imagine and create during our lifetimes right here and now. Take a moment and allow that to sink in.

At the center of every society is a story. Where we came from, who we are, and where we are going collectively are at the heart of these narratives. By buying into the stories, we can establish trust with people we've never met because *they* believe the same story. There was a story at the center of Babylon, Sparta, Athens, and Rome. Likewise, there is a story at the center of America, Russia, and China. There is a story at the center of every successful business you've ever heard of from Apple to Microsoft. Everything and everyone has a story. Nothing under the sun is *about nothing.*

To a certain scale of population, folklore and superstition are enough to cement a population together. These are the stories that you would tell around the campfire to scare children or to teach life lessons. As the society grows, however, more people from different cultures are exposed to one another, and stories alone are not enough. Many stories must be compiled and concisely organized into an epic of some kind. Every culture in the world has achieved this through some form of religion.

The word *religion* has been traditionally associated with the supernatural and the spiritual. This is a narrow view of the word, not to mention a complete misinterpretation. Capitalism is just as much a religion as Christianity, as well as any form of Marxism, Liberalism, or Fascism. Any story that has a concisely organized narrative is, by definition, a religion.

"Religion" from the Greek, translates literally to "ligament." Just as the ligaments in your knees and ankles hold the various muscles and bones stable, religion packages *values* together into a narrative-driven system that can then be expressed and accepted by a wide variety of people. The more people that the story can appeal to, the more power it holds.

Throughout the various religions, the same rules are often expressed: don't lie, don't steal, don't seek revenge, don't rape, and for the love of God, leave your neighbor's wife alone. In general, don't do anything that would otherwise limit the function of your society by disturbing the peace. Just as there is no room for jealousy or greed in a hunter-gatherer group, there is only so much room within society for discord before the society itself crumbles.

These systems of rules become compiled and expressed in codes of behavior. The Ten Commandments of the Bible, the Code of Hammurabi, the system of Bushido in feudal Japan, and the Nangwali Code are all examples of these systems of ethical behavior, and they have the ability to influence the behavior of millions of people at once. Some people don't follow the rules, of course, and they are often made an example for their "sins.". Either they are executed publicly, or they are carted off to the fringes (otherwise known as prisons, work camps, furnaces, etc.)

Whether you believe literally in it or not, religion is a story, and stories drive human behavior and allow us to find common ground. You can be a full-fledged atheist, but if you live in Saudi Arabia, much of your behavior will be dictated by the teachings of the Koran, while in the United States you are influenced more by the Bible than you might like to admit. It doesn't matter where you came from, or even what language you speak. If you and I believe in the natural rights of human beings, or the narratives of the Bhagavad Gita or the Bible, we can then participate together in the same cultural rituals such as church and Sabbath, the celebration of Eid, or the Day of the Dead.

Likewise, if you and I believe in major slogans, such as "manifest destiny" or "Operation Enduring Freedom," we can both participate in these struggles, further advancing the cause of whatever we are doing.

Because we experience these rites together, we can trust each other. Because we can trust one another, the door for larger-scale cooperation swings wide open, and large-scale trade agreements can exist. Only then can an empire stand strong.

The "Greatest" Story Ever Told (So Far)

When you look at a dollar bill, you are looking at something with absolutely no intrinsic value. Indeed, the dollar bill is little more than a decorated piece of toilet paper without the belief backing its value. You can't eat it, nor can you drink it. And yet, because of a few incredible story-tellers and their ability to persuade people to buy in, the power a dollar holds is undeniable.

Money is, in fact, a story, and it's currently the most successful story that's ever been told. This is evident of how money transcends cultural boundaries. Not everyone believes in the accounts of Genesis nor in the chronicles presented in the Ramayana. In fact, sharply drawn boundaries exist upon the lines of these religious narratives, driving conflict across the globe.

In contrast, virtually everyone living in modern society believes in the value of money. You might despise it. You might even think it's the root of all evil, but if a hundred dollars is handed to you, the possibilities of your day become immediately more expansive.

The value of money is in its ability to simplify the process of transacting goods by acting as a universal unit of conversion. We take it for granted that we no longer have to think about the conversion rates of our goods and services, but without this crucial technology, business would be a daily headache.

Let's Go Back in Time

You live in a small kingdom of interconnected towns that survive through mutual interest in trade. You are a metal worker, specializing in fine swords and armor for the local militia. You need to buy bread for your family, so you walk into town to the local bakery. You offer your skill to craft a knife for the baker in order to trade for the food you need. The baker, however, has everything he needs and declines your offer. He also knows you specialize in swords and might think your knife-making technique is subpar. Maybe there is another metal-worker in town who is better at that particular implement. Your skill and trade are then rendered ineffective in getting you what you need. *Womp, womp.* What do you do? Perhaps he needs instead a new pair of leather gloves.

You venture over to the leather worker and offer him a fine sword. Thank God, you think, when he agrees. Turns out, he's feuding with one of the local pub owners over an overdue bar tab. The poor guy would like a little extra security by his bedside. He gives you the pair of gloves in exchange for your promise to craft him the sword within two weeks. You then take the gloves to the baker, who then gives you a bag of bread. All in all, you managed to secure bread for your family, but it took you the better part of the day to do so, not to mention a few weeks of work to craft the sword, if you actually do deliver the product. In essence, you probably have only dumb luck to thank for what is only temporary success.

Now imagine the same scenario but with a system of coins. Instead of trading and bartering your craft throughout town, you can focus exclusively on manufacturing for the local militia. You work in exchange for a few copper coins for each blade. You can then take those coins to the baker who charges you a fixed rate of two coins for a bag of bread, and you even have a few other coins for fruits and vegetables. You're on your way back home for breakfast before the sun is even up, whistling a happy tune as you walk.

It's hard to overstate the importance currency has had in the history of human beings, especially as societies grew. For most of history, the archetypal stories of the Bible, the Koran, and the Gita influenced on a major scale how humans behaved. This worked regionally because humans of different belief systems rarely had to congregate.

Over the last few centuries, however, as worldwide travel and trade became more common, entire cultures have been thrown into the midst of others. Christian capitalists began to do business in Bushido Japan, while Hindus in India began to trade more with Buddhists in Tibet. The same pattern presents itself over and over again throughout the increasingly globalizing world. When people of different religious ideologies are forced to congregate, their traditional beliefs are no longer enough to cement the new arrangements. New, more expansive narratives need to be created.

Modern society itself is predicated more upon the economic systems at play than it is in how the society orients itself spiritually. This is because the stories present within economics bind more people together than spiritual orientation. In the modern world, it matters less whether you're a Christian or Buddhist than if you're a capitalist or communist.

Most Americans might profess love of Jesus Christ, but would they do the same if it meant giving up pensions, their houses, the food on their table, or the clothes on their back? The reality is no. Most will pay lip-service each Sunday to their deity of choice; however, when the chips are down, most will choose their economic prosperity and security over their faith in their God. I say this not to be disrespectful, only to illustrate the reality at hand.

The traditional religions such as Hinduism, Islam, and Christianity are simply not enough in their entirety to hold a global society together. They have become more like fringe decoration pieces rather than the center-pieces that bring the dinner table together. This is not a good thing. At least the traditional religions have spirit. Worship of money has none.

The Twentieth Century

Were you to fall asleep and wake up in the 1920s, you would be told one of three stories about the world. Were you to open your eyes in Moscow, you'd be eating Marxist ideology for breakfast, lunch, and dinner. Liberalism would be your daily bread in New York City, and if you happened to be in Berlin or Tokyo, you'd eventually run into fascism whether it be in support of the Third Reich or the Imperial regime.

The grim history of the twentieth century can be boiled down to the massive social experiments that were these three new-world religions. None of them, however, have anything to do with how humans view God. Each of them are predicated upon economics and social identity.

Liberalism is the belief that liberty and freedom are paramount in society. In communism, equality is at the top, and fascism is the belief that your country's story is the *only* relevant story. The fascist regime will often elevate its history and race above all others, such as the belief, for example, that Aryan Germans were the pure-blood, master race of the world. *All others*, says the fascist, *are beneath us.*

Naturally, all three of these ideologies grind against one another. War becomes inevitable on a global scale. And come it did.

The Socially Violent Ape

War is perhaps as old as the Hominid genus itself. Many of our ape cousins routinely practice violence towards one another. Jane Goodall, the legendary eco-researcher, was disturbed and heartbroken to see the violent behavior of the chimps she studied. If, for example, a troupe of chimps came across a loner that was not part of the group, they would beat the loner to death without mercy. Whole groups commit genocide against others, and so on.

While we as a species don't fully identify taxonomically with chimps (we're just as close to the bonobos), many of the early human tribes were just as warlike as any warring nation of the modern world. The only difference is in scale. It would be a mistake to think that foraging tribes were all peace-loving and friendly towards one another. War was practiced by many tribes, along with the rituals that develop as conflict grows. In addition, tribes practiced various forms of torture that were sickening for the average modern mind to contemplate. To those unlucky souls to be captured alive by the enemy, the fate was often being hacked to pieces in ritual ceremony, roasted over a fire, or simply fed alive to the dogs.

We take it for granted in the modern world that we generally don't have to be worry about being captured and butchered to death. This simply wasn't the case for much of human history.

As awful as war is and the brutal behavior that it can inspire in humans, it has often been the most immediate and practical glue that held our societies together as they expanded and the binds between citizens severed. It is an illusion that any society can live in perennial peace. Religion and currency, for all their worth, are sometimes not enough. It's very possible indeed that kings and politicians of the past and present have rationalized their constituency into conflict with other nations if only to prevent a conflict at home.

A great example of this is the United States. Throughout the last two centuries, the country has been continually ravaged by conflict within its own borders. Aside from gang violence itself, mass killings (those that are defined by four or more people dying in an incident) have been a constant scourge throughout the last century. The interesting thing is that mass killings and gang violence actually decreased during both World Wars, and far from degrading the production of the economy, war has been shown to actually increase production and inspire growth within a nation. That growth also tends to come from a boost in morale that can be attributed to a greater feeling of unity within the war-time population. "Times were better when things were hell," as the saying goes, "and war is hell, baby."

War galvanizes each citizen into a shared necessity for survival because it directly and indirectly traumatizes a population as a whole, from the platoon to the society level. Bombings kill the politician as easily as they kill the poor. The effect of this concentrates the community effort into a fixed goal. War raises the stakes: "*We must defeat them, or they will kill us <u>all</u>.*" Even worse, *they* might rape our women and sell our children as slaves (See virtually all of human history.).

War also has the benefit of traumatizing all demographics alike. The London Blitz killed the rich as effectively as it killed the poor and as many blacks as it did whites. It didn't matter what demographic you were. War traumatizes all, and within that trauma, people bind together in the name of necessity.

Even as the world watched while the American government launched a full-scale bombing campaign that killed tens of thousands of Afghans, a sense of American pride actually went up in the years following 9/11. Murder rates and violent crime went *down*. Likewise, during the London Blitz of World War II, social ties were strengthened and the war-time economy actually improved in the UK. Imagine it - much of your business and industry infrastructure is being targeted and destroyed, and yet you're still showing improvement. The same was true later when the Allies bombed Germany. The more they bombed, the harder the resolve of the Germans became against the Allies.

You see the same pattern when natural disasters strike…when volcanos erupt, tsunamis hit, and rivers flood. The devastation is immediate and felt by everyone involved. Through the shared trauma, the people affected band together, social classes disappear, and welfare for the group becomes forefront.

All of this, of course, factored into the bloodiest century in human history. Within the folds of their societies, people didn't pay attention to what was now the obvious barbarity of the Third Reich, nor did your average Japanese citizen see the brutality of the imperialist regime for which they labored. They simply became intoxicated by the vision and security that these groups embodied, and the glorious stories they were no doubt propagating.

This is something for the modern human being to contemplate. Once upon a time, due to our bias towards belonging, people just like you and I subscribed to tyranny and brutal conquest. And as we'll see later, the twenty-first century is no different. Humans are up to much of the same shit, only in a different era.

Back to the Twentieth Century

Two World Wars, several holocausts, many millions of people butchered at war, another one hundred million starved and frozen in the Soviet gulags, and thousands of grisly forms of human experimentation throughout Manchuria. All of this was to decide which global narrative would prevail. Fascism all but died out after World War II. Turns out that elevating your country above all others set the stage for a rather disturbing chain of events in the countries that exhibited it: concentration camps in Germany and Imperial Japanese abuse throughout China all but put the final nail in the coffin for fascism. Communism fell largely with the fall of the Soviet Union, and since then the vast majority of the countries in the world have been members of the liberal story.

Authority lies with the consumer in the liberal story. We see liberalism in how we conduct business, how we manufacture products, and how we educate the members of our society.

Take, for example, automobiles. In a communist state, a few powerful individuals will get together and decide on how the product should be made. *A car*, they might say, *should be durable, compact, and able to transport up to four people over no more than forty kilometers daily.* They will then manufacture hundreds of thousands of such vehicles for everyone. If anyone has a problem with the vehicle, it is *their* problem, not the government's.

In contrast, in a liberal society such as the United States, walk onto any car lot and you'll find a vast spectrum of vehicle designs, not to mention colors and customizations. Fuel efficient cars for commuting, gas guzzling trucks for farm work, mini-vans for the soccer mom, and SUVs for whomever cares to pay the money for them. You will never see a car dealership insist that "everyone needs *this* car," and refuse to deal with all other automobiles. Short of a very compelling and kick-ass ad campaign, they'll simply be out of business in a liberal society.

A liberal story maintains that the consumer is king. How she spends her dollars is how her world is shaped. As consumers, we hold the reins. We can decide what gets manufactured, which technology is developed, and how it is used. In reality, this is a very heavy amount of responsibility, spread out through a population that exercises no general dialogue in "how to vote," so to speak. Because humans are biased towards pleasure and convenience, how we are currently shaping society is directly against the needs of our biology. We see this in the technological revolution of the twenty-first century. Three decades ago, nobody knew how to even send an email. Such a trick was the domain of the eccentric super-nerd. Now we live in a world where you and I are connected at all times to a vast system of commerce. Because of how we're using this new super-technology, we could be killing ourselves and eroding the very foundations of our societies.

Social Media: A Deep Dive into Shallow Waters

It's been over thirty years since Tim Berners-Lee wrote the code for the world-wide web. Since then, the Internet has become the main medium by which information is received by human beings, replacing all other mediums such as books, radio, and television. It's hard to overstate the advantages of the Internet. Having ready access to such a vast and organized amount of data has every reason to be applauded. I'm convinced that I've done at least half of the research for this very book through watching TED Talks and reading peer-reviewed studies on the web. The other half was done through reading books, all of which I researched on Google before buying.

Search engines such as Google offer an immense value to society because they concentrate and organize information and ideas that once required pain-staking labor to find separately. Even twenty years ago, college research required hours spent searching for the required book in a library. Once you found the book, hours more were required skimming the pages before you found the required passage that had the information you needed. By typing your question into Google instead, the search engine connects you to the information you need in moments.

The Internet has reunited family members, found blood and organ donors, and spread awareness about holistic and worthwhile causes around the world. It's been a blessing to society. But as the Greek Sophocles once said, "Nothing vast enters the lives of mortals without also bringing a curse."

Depending on how you use social media, there is a night and day effect. You have a tool that can streamline your business, connect you with people like you all around the world, and you even have a platform to grow your brand faster than at any other time in history. And yet, due to how we are currently using social media, depression and suicide rates are skyrocketing, especially in teenagers. Political polarity seems to be worsening, and the age of information seems to have turned into the age of dis-information. How do humans stick together when each individual has access to their own bias?

Who is the Tool?

Most of your social media platforms like Facebook, Instagram, and Twitter run on an advertisement-based business model. If you've ever wondered why these services are free, why you don't pay for YouTube videos, or the ability to have your own profile on IG or Twitter, this is why. If you don't pay for a product, what that usually means is that *you are the product.* The money for these platforms come from advertising by companies who want a platform on which to show their products and services. Companies like Coca Cola and GM pay Instagram or YouTube to air ads for their products. The product, in this case then, is not you but your attention. How much of your attention do you give to these platforms?

On the other side of every cell phone and computer screen is a team of engineers and millions of computers running vastly complicated algorithms, all of which have a goal in mind. A computer algorithm can be thought of as an opinion encoded into a system. Algorithms are programmed with an end goal in mind.

In this case, it's usually to make money for the companies who program them. The three objectives of most social platforms are Engagement, Growth, and Monetization. Engagement: how much time can the platform get you to give? Growth: how many new users will you bring back? Monetization: how much money can ultimately be generated by the collective engagement?

Because everything you do online is saved and monitored, these algorithms know you better than most of your friends. They know your name, where you live, your sexual orientation, your tastes in music and art, and what groups you belong to. Based on this collected data, they then can offer you advertisements for products you might like. This is how the Amazon algorithm seems to know to send you a recommendation for that book or album you've been thinking about, or how the Twitter algorithm knows to connect you with a particular group based on the trending ideology of your posts.

You have to ask yourself: are you using social media or is it using you?

Searching for Depth

The overall structure of the brain hasn't changed much over the last seventy thousand years. Beneath the shape itself, however, is a different story. The millions of neurons within the brain are in constant change, adapting to the collective lifestyles of the humans they inhabit. Technology has always had a radical change on how we think, behave, and communicate, as well as the different neural connections that come with such change.

Whether we're talking about the development of writing and mathematics or inventions like the printing press or the radio, each of these new technologies changed the constructs of the culture surrounding them. Because human beings behaved differently, their brains changed to facilitate the new behavior.

As we've adopted computer technology for most of our media source, we've slowly lost what used to be our old linear thought process. Usually this would be connected with reading, that feeling you get when you get so deep into a book that you become "lost within the print."

Nicolas Carr writes in *The Shallow*, "When we go online, we enter an environment that promotes cursory reading, hurried and distracted thinking, and superficial learning." When we go online, we are bombarded by notifications, and our attention is pulled from one video to another in the seemingly endless stream of media. Because we must navigate the environment of the web, the pre-frontal cortex fires up, and the executive function of the brain kicks in.

Conversely, a book seems to represent a deep sea; patient, quiet, waiting for your attention. Your computer and iPhone are more like an errant child, demanding your attention through a raging torrent of notifications that are constantly chiming. The Internet seizes our attention only to scatter it. Our ability to focus becomes dubious at best, and our ability to empathize and communicate become shallow. Finding depth in such an environment is out of the question. This is at a crucial point in history when global problems are forcing us into a situation where we must be able to communicate effectively and deeply.

Ninety percent of communication happens via non-verbal cues, yet we live in a world where the vast majority of communication happens via text message. As of 2010, the average teenager was sending over three thousand text messages per month. When we've lost the ability to empathize and achieve depth in real time with one another, we become less able to deal with the problems that are prevalent within our societies. This inability to empathize and connect has happened at a moment in time when we are facing grave dangers as a global society. Technology, rather than helping us, seems to be making our problems worse. Because of the advertisement-based business model, the companies only make money when they can seize your attention. It turns out that the thing people most love to see is that which reconfirms their own bias.

Post-Truth: The Great Divide

There's no doubt that social media has given us a greater opportunity for connection. Through platforms like Instagram and Twitter, you can live on completely different continents and still keep in touch with friends and family in your home country. As I'm writing this, I'm living in the United States, yet I maintain connections with friends in countries like Brazil, France, and Indonesia via WhatsApp.

All of this connection, however, is overshadowed by social media's ability to unite us *against* one another. Facebook, for example, has been accused throughout the last decade of being used to sew discord within countries and influence democratic elections through the spread of fake news. And it turns out that the consequences of fake news lead to real problems in the world.

In Miramar, hundreds of thousands of Muslims were forced to flee the country after mass genocide and rape broke out upon the minority. In the final analysis, the genocides began due to fake news stories circulating about a Muslim man raping a Buddhist woman. In 2013, a different scenario unfolded in Egypt where President Hosni Mubarak was forced to step down from office after millions of people stood against him on a Facebook group. After the president stepped down, the group itself celebrated the victory before breaking into many different groups, all fighting amongst one another for control of the country. It pays to mention that each group broken off from the original had a Facebook page to represent itself, and each page passed on its own version of propaganda.

There is Something Distinctly Different Here

You can easily argue that fake news has always existed and that this is but another stepping stone. Perhaps you're right. Propaganda has always existed. Humans are a post-truth species. As commented earlier, our ability to cooperate on a massive scale requires our ability to invent stories and imbue them with meaning. Above one hundred and fifty members in any given tribe, and gossip alone is unable to solve the issues of gluing the populace together. Stories must replace reality. Fake news, then, has existed since the Stone Age. We call it religion.

I believe the current situation we find ourselves in is different because of the effectiveness of the tools. Never has technology like Facebook existed for would-be influencers to "educate" the masses. If I want to manipulate you, for example, all I have to do is find a fault line in society. Pro-life/pro-choice is an example. The topic is a powder keg, just waiting to be lit. From here, I create two fake accounts on Facebook: one against abortion and another that is for it. Once I create the two pages, I can then invite people that I know to the two pages, and from behind the fake accounts, I can post articles and videos that validate the theme of whichever site. If I'm good at what I'm doing, I can amass a following of millions of people on both sites and further drive a wedge between the demographics that the fake accounts symbolize. Because the Facebook algorithm has no ability to tell fact from fiction, it actually aids me in polarizing the two groups. It's only goal is to create growth. So, because fake news is more enticing, it is what the algorithm decides to spread, and because the Internet is so vast, we have no way of fact-checking all of the news stories that come through our feeds. Because we can't agree on what is true and what isn't, we fail to find common ground.

Cracks in the Mirror

Fault lines have always existed in society. Different people come with different life experiences. This is natural. However, once a line is sharply drawn between any two viewpoints, it's crucial that there remain debate and discussion between the opposing extremes. A society that does not share discourse along its fault lines will become more polarized. The fault lines will begin to move farther apart, and the views of the opposing sides will become more extreme. When this happens, the intent of the conflict becomes less about what is good for the people's welfare as a whole, but instead on the domination over the opposing group. In such a state, the society will slowly churn itself into chaos.

How does such a process start in real life? A good example is the contempt so prevalent between opposing party members in the United States. The fault lines are such that identity politics is the norm, defined as identifying only with the group that shares and reinforces your viewpoint. Based on your views on any given subject, you are immediately grouped into an intellectual boat. "You're pro-choice," a conservative says in disgust. "Another baby-killing democrat."

Three things are implicit in the statements of such people. The first is that they rarely, if ever, encounter a person that opposes their viewpoints, indicating a limited identity. The second is their inability to see a spectrum within the opposing sides, assuming a general picture of the entire group. The third, and most horrifying for what it implies down the road, is the assumption of *moral superiority over the opposing group.*

History has Taught us What Happens
Once We Walk Down this Road

Once humans assume moral superiority, they become capable of unfathomable cruelty towards one another. The Jesuits assumed moral superiority over the indigenous throughout the globe. The Nazis assumed it over the Jews, and the Japanese assumed it over the Chinese. Look what happened: state-sponsored rape, murder, infanticide, human experimentation, burning at the stake, and every other species of atrocity became so normalized that it was sometimes broadcasted for the world to see.

Moral superiority is the beginning of the end. Conflict and abuse become inevitable. As the dominos begin to fall, they pick up speed and there's no turning back. Revolutions emerge, civil wars erupt, countless are killed, revenge culture grows like a cancer, and the vicious cycle continues until there's nothing but the ash from the last receding flame.

In the United States, both of the two parties routinely and openly revile one another. Open discourse along the fault lines rarely exists, and when it does, it's usually to trap an opposing viewpoint into a harrowing scene of degradation aired to viewers worldwide. Even within the parties themselves, a large spectrum exists. Whether the subject is minority rights, sexual orientation, or religious belief, debates rage between people of opposing viewpoints, each person taking the "moral high ground" so that society becomes fragmented more and more over time. How many cracks can appear in the mirror before it shatters? And how long until war erupts throughout society, tearing to pieces the cultural fabric that gave it birth?

Look at what's currently happening in many American cities. Protests, riots, and police brutality are becoming so normal that stories in the news stay for only a day or two before being replaced by another grizzly occurrence. The domestic war currently raging throughout the United States is much more complicated than a North vs. South Civil War dynamic. The conflict is much more multi-faceted, and there are many more players in the game. Whites are fighting blacks. Gays are fighting the straight, conservatives fighting liberals, and the media seems to be at war with everybody. This makes it incredibly difficult for any politician trying to reign control of their traditionally-united constituency.

Where do you even begin to break down such problems?

Safety Within the Group

The modern American is one of three and fifty million people. India and China both number in populations of a billion. Even countries like that of the European Union boast population sizes within the tens of millions. The fact that these people are organized beneath the same political banner implies that they operate towards a fixed goal collectively. But do they? A quick glance at the news betrays otherwise.

The world is a globalized entity. Something that happens in Silicon Valley has an effect in Bangalore. What happens in the West has an effect on what happens in Africa. And though the economy of the world is largely globalized, we are still playing an outdated game of nationalistic politics. People are still under the illusion that their country can be completely independent from all others. Yet a quick survey of the things you enjoy every day tell a completely different story. The coffee you drink is probably from Brazil or Guatemala, the metals that go into your smart phone and computers were mined in the Democratic Republic of Congo, and the gas you're putting into your tank comes from various conglomerates in the Middle East.

While the countries of the world have grown increasingly inter-dependent upon one another, they've failed to update the stories that they tell their citizens. It makes little sense to identify only with your nation of birth when you are depending on people a world away for almost every facet of your lifestyle.

In the vast, sprawling expanse of society, there is safety within identifying with a group. The identity politics that we're seeing worldwide could very well be a reaction to social platforms that are simply too expansive for our nervous systems to digest. Humans are social creatures, but only at a very local level. Most of our history was characterized by population densities of a few hundred people at most. Your typical hunter-gatherer band follows the same trend, rarely living in groups more than a few hundred people. Over two hundred thousand years were spent in this way. We are wired for group interests, which is why groups like ISIS can exist. In an often shallow, technology-driven world, they offer people a genuine tribe, even if the tribe itself has sinister intent towards the rest of the world.

What's Good for Us Will Be the End of Us

While we are indeed wired for the tribe, we live in a world where nuclear war can become reality with but one slip of the finger. Living tribally, then, that which is shown to be very healthy for our nervous systems is the very thing that will kill us as a whole. What are we to do in a world of rapid globalization? How do we craft a narrative that allows us to live in the deep-seated community that we need while also embracing an ever-expansive social identity? How do you work for the welfare of your family and community while also acting with humanity towards the other groups outside of our own?

Crafting a Global Narrative

We have no idea how AI technology will change the world, nor do we have a clue how block chain technology will revamp economics. All we know is that a massive shift is coming, and if we are to survive it, we must unite. Collectively, humanity faces climate change, over-population, deforestation, nuclear war, and environmental collapse, all of which we currently have no collective answers to.

Though we are all tied into a globalized economy, we still have one hundred and ninety-five sovereign nations that are acting individually through nationalistic politics. In such a state, we can't even begin to address the issues that we face. If, for example, the United States bans deforestation tomorrow, nothing changes in countries like China or Brazil. Because nothing changes worldwide, the clock still ticks, heading towards eco-logical disaster.

The fond nostalgia for nationalism is one based in delusion and fear of the unknown. The world is different than it was in the twentieth century. We've used technology to create a world in which we have three main threats, each of which can't be solved through national policy. Nuclear war, climate change, and technological disruption will have an effect on humanity as a whole.

Patriotism is not the problem. There is no shame in being proud of being an American, nor is there in proclaiming yourself

South African, Russian, German, etc. Nationalistic chauvinism, however, the idea that your country reigns supreme, will stand in the way of solving the problems that we face. As long as individual nations put their interests first before that of the world's, we will leave ourselves incapable of dealing with what is coming. Keep your pride. But never forget that you are a human before you are a part of your nation.

The Liberal Problem

Liberalism, for all its success throughout the last century, can't solve the global problems we face. In fact, it exacerbates them. Liberalism is fueled by economic growth, but as Harari points out in *21 Lessons for the 21st Century*, "Economic growth is the cause of the eco-logical crisis. And economic growth will not solve technological disruption, because it is predicated on the invention of more and more disruptive technologies."

Liberalism, then, will either have to reinvent itself or give way to a broader, more enlightened narrative. But what will that narrative be, and why is it so important now?

In the past, societies were regional, changing slowly over a course of generations. When a society failed, it was only felt by the people within the region. In contrast, the society that you and I are a part of is global. Think about it: the Internet alone has revolutionized everything from how humans conduct business, communicate, and even how we socialize and pursue sex in a span of twenty years. Furthermore, the Internet has effectively flattened the world, allowing companies to streamline and outsource their work at an increased rate. We're more united than ever, but there is no regulating authority presiding over that reality.

The mere mention of a world order spawns ideas of dystopian societies where the average person lives in fear and suffering, surveyed relentlessly by a tyrannical government. It's no surprise, especially in the West. Immortalized literature like *1984* and *Brave New World* have effectively burned into the psyche of every reader, a perfectly reasonable fear of any globalized authority.

How is a thing like this even possible in the first place? What central theme do you instill at the center? Is it an authoritarian government where a single leader calls the shots? Are we to live in a worldwide communist dictatorship? How could socialism be effective in this scheme? Is it even possible to have a democracy? Furthermore, what about religion? Which of the major religions in the world will be chosen as the corner piece? Christianity or Islam? What about Hinduism or Buddhism? Where do they find their place within the grand melting pot?

The reality is that each religion and each central theme will need to lend a hand. A global narrative would have to include a combination of all the different themes and religious belief systems. This is no easy task because it means that some of the foundational principles of religions such as Christianity and Islam will have to be discarded. The widespread notion throughout the Abrahamic tradition that books like the Bible, Koran, and Talmud hold the only sources of real truth will have to be put to rest and open up to the possibility that other religions have something to offer.

Biology lends a hand to crafting the narrative by telling us two definite things about human beings: the first is that we are dependent upon ecological systems for a very finite number of resources. Even as you're breathing, you're depending on the trees around you who produce oxygen as a bio-product of their lives. The food you eat, the water you drink, even the fossil fuels that you pump into your car engine. These are all finite resources that were created within the planet we live upon. Once we use them up, we die.

The second is that humans are incredibly social creatures, but only at the local level. We evolved to exist within tribes of one hundred and fifty people or so. Any global narrative that we create going further into the twenty-first century will have to start with these two foundational stones. From these twain, all else will be additions. The religions will have to conform to them exactly if they hope to remain.

Along with the narrative, we will have to decide the role that technology will play in reshaping how we live. How will we allow artificial intelligence to work for us? Will we let the technology completely take over the work of our society? How will this affect our relations with one another? Furthermore, how do we allow social media to play a role in our lives? Is there a way to use these things for the good of human beings, or are we doomed to fight against algorithms until they ultimately control us?

The Global Discussions

In short, there's no panel of discussion for a united humanity. For this, we must return to the time-honored traditions of discussion and debate. As a Westerner, I have my ideas for a global narrative, but they tend to be biased towards capitalism and Christianity to show the way. These are the things I grew up with, and they are what I'm most familiar with. Personal bias cast aside, however, they present obvious problems.

A first principle of capitalism is growth, and this has many benefits. But a society must always ask itself what it is growing for. If capitalism is only in service to growth for the sake of growth, then having the biggest GDP, the best score upon the score board of global competition…there is no meaning here. It doesn't address the issues of welfare within society.

Take Brazil, for example: a worldwide leader in meat packaging, the country is one of the richest in the world if we are to look at GDP. One walk through a *favela* in Rio De Janeiro, however, will disillusion you to the fact that it's a truly *prosperous* country.

If capitalism can't find a way to consider welfare of the people along with growth, the society will be doomed to collapse. This is true of any nation that values its economy over the well-being of its people.

Christianity has its own set of problems as history has shown: Christianity is a monotheistic religion, which has no room for other belief systems, other gods, and other perspectives. It simply doesn't have the ability to reconcile differences between different people of different origins. A history of brutality and torture towards non-believers has all but confirmed this.

In the same hand, Christianity comes with a deep fault within its own narrative and in how it predicts the end of the world. Other religions do this, of course. Since the dawn of human consciousness, humans have been spinning elaborate tales about the origin of the world, along with its inevitable end. Science itself has verified this. Earth will not go on forever. The ozone layer will leave, our sun will expand, what is presumably a black hole at the center of our galaxy will swallow us up, etc. The earth will not last forever, period.

It's not that Judeo-Christian belief predicts the end of the world as all others belief systems do, it is that the nature of the narrative causes believers to actually *look forward* to the end of times. In their minds, it means deliverance for them, fire and flames for others. Christianity comes with a self-destruct button, if only for the sake of confirming its own prophetic bias.

Self-Fulfilling Prophecies

Prophecies can be a royal son of a bitch. Imagine something that may not even be realistic initially. Because a massive amount of people believe in it, it not only becomes possible, but *inevitable*.

Belief becomes reality when we speak of human beings. As discussed earlier, *humans imagine futures, and those futures then become reality*. If an entire society views the end of the world to be near, the psychological impulse of each person will be such that they will act in ways that bring about the predicted outcome. I've had to endure many discussions with believers of the Judeo-Christian traditions, not to mention Hindus, Buddhists, and Pagans who believe many of the same ideas. Speaking of problems throughout the world, these discussions inevitably lead to someone saying, "Well, it's the end of times. There's nothing we can do. It's prophecy." They'll then narrate whatever particular prophecy is implicated by *their* text. "Armageddon will happen, it says so in the Bible." If this is true, then, from a Christian perspective, the end of times have been coming for the last two thousand years since the death of Christ. Even the life of Christ itself was eventually inevitable *because* it was predicted for thousands of years, acting as an emotional coping mechanism for the Jewish populations suffering under the heels of superiors who held them under bonds.

It takes very little imagination to see that some of these people actually *look* forward to the end of the world, if only to be able to say, "I told you so," in the end. And yet, if you believe the end of times is *always* coming, then you can't possibly be wrong when it finally does. Forget the fact that you've been saying the same shit for two thousand years now. "Jesus is coming!" Yeah, I heard you a millennia ago, brother.

Just because you can't possibly be wrong doesn't make you necessarily right. And in the end, it becomes largely irrelevant that you actually *caused* the end of times. Thus, the doomsday prophecy is really nothing more than a self-fulfilling prophecy, freeing humans from the responsibility of preserving the world that they are currently destroying. When the world seems to be falling apart, it's much easier to give it to God than it is to take real action. Humans act how they believe, and in an interesting feedback loop, those actions create further sustaining belief on *how* to act.

And though Christianity has obvious problems in regards to crafting a global narrative, we should be very careful not to throw the baby out with the bathwater. The narratives within the Bible offer deeply profound and redeemable answers for how human beings should live, but for the above reasons, the Bible shouldn't be used to craft a global society.

Religion cannot continue to exist if it insists that it knows the answers that it clearly doesn't. Clever though we may be, we humans don't even understand matter at the smallest level. If you look at an atom, you will find a proton and neutron fused, while an electron circles the pair. Ninety-nine percent of the space that comprises an atom is empty space, and we are only just now beginning to explore that space.

To believe something is to insist upon a notion despite ignorance. We have only a vague idea scientifically of the nature of reality, yet we have religious zealots running around the world proclaiming their own brand of creationism. Because the nature of religion is speculation, buying into any particular religion or ideology is a practice of ignorance. Instead of being open to possibility, you become closed down to your fellow human beings, and over something so trivial at the root. It is as though you've bought a thousand piece puzzle, but you've been given only three pieces of the product. We do not even know a grain of sand in its entirety, yet with our three pieces of the puzzle, we arrange a picture and decide *this is life*. Rubbish.

Far more sinister, however, is the byproduct that is created by religious belief – that of separation.

The Illusion of Separation

Despite scientific evidence to the contrary, modern humans still seem thoroughly convinced that they are separate entities, particularly along the fault lines of their own countries and religion. Separation is an illusion. From a biological point of view, the only thing that separates you from any other human being is but a minute percentage of DNA variants. From a sociological point of view, as we've discussed, you depend, in many cases, more on foreigners for your lifestyle than you do on your own countrymen. I'll give you an example: if every farmer in Colombia, Costa Rica, Guatemala, and Brazil were unable to continue their work raising cacao and coffee beans, every American would be out of their morning joe within a few short weeks. That is the world we live in - one of inter-dependence. Anyone who tells you differently simply isn't looking at the big picture.

At the root of every atrocity ever committed is the illusion of separation. We must craft a world in which every human sees that they are connected. Until that time of enlightenment, we'll continue to circle the drain, until the earth rids itself of us permanently.

A Different Way

Modern social life among humans is currently defined by ignorance and fear. This is because we think we already know the answers due to our belief systems. In order to turn the table, we must each decide on a different path - that of the seeker. You see this in children. They are naturally curious. You will rarely find a child that will profess to you the nature of the world. This behavior is taught. To be a seeker is to not buy in too much to your impressions of the world and instead explore the possibilities for yourself. Only then will you be free of the oppressive ignorance that is ideology, and only when humans do this collectively will we begin to move forward.

Foundational Stone of a Global Narrative

Many thousands of years ago, hundreds of small hunter-gatherer tribes lived along a bountiful river. Theirs was a country of desert, subject to incredible heat during the summer months. The river, however, provided a more temperate climate, complete with dense jungle and the bountiful produce that is characteristic of such an environment. Though the tribes themselves didn't get along, they subsisted upon the same source of nourishment living along the river. If one part of the river experienced a sudden food shortage or natural catastrophe, the tribe that inhabited that part of the river would have no help. Most likely, they'd parish.

Eventually, tribal leaders perceived the wisdom of cooperating with other tribes. Trade agreements were established, and people from different tribes traveled more often up and down the river leading to mixed relations between tribes. Eventually, a unified community sprung up in the name of necessity. Fast forward to modern day, and we now know that river as the Nile. We know that ancient community as the Egyptian Empire. When humans work together, the possibilities are endless. The tribes along the Nile were only able to work together in unison once they could *perceive* the needs of the other communities around them, and this is important.

The story of ancient Egypt is, of course, the same story that has repeated itself for the last ten thousand years. It is the story of how thousands of individual tribes ultimately came to rest here in the twenty-first century where there exist around two hundred sovereign nations. The stakes in the modern world, however, are much higher.

Whereas each tribe of that pre-Egyptian Nile faced its problems alone, humans of the modern world face our global issues *together* whether we like it or not. Global warming will hurt China as much as the United States. Environmental pollution will eventually poison the people of Buenos Aires as easily as it does in Flint, Michigan. We can stay apart and die, or we can face these issues on a united front.

Ask yourself this: when you see a photo of a Chinese person or a child starving in Afghanistan, can you feel sympathy? Can you relinquish your reflexive national chauvinism and, in the end, perceive that it's another *human being* staring back at you? Despite what your government officials are telling you, we live on this one planet *together*. For now, forget all the long-winded speeches of a unified government. Remember, first, that we are all human. In forming a global society, we can begin here.

Sex

Horny Apes

Nobody, short of artificial means, is alive today without sex. Every person you know is a product of copulation. Your parents had sex, probably many times, before *you* were conceived. If this makes you uncomfortable, you should stop reading now. If you're offended in the first paragraph alone, imagine what awaits you in the next twenty pages.

For those of you who decide to stay with me - buckle up. The ride is about to get bumpy.

The Beast with Two Backs

Yes, your parents had sex. So did mine. As a result, I'm here writing a book while you're here reading, perhaps even being traumatized by it. For better or worse, that is our reality as we sit here on this rock orbiting through the darkness of space. Yet somehow, when it comes to sex, we're all so screwed up in the head that we feel dazed and disoriented on the subject, while the most neurotic of us live out a drama as compelling as any soap opera.

If you're like me, you were lucky enough to have a significant other tell you that you were horrible at sex. This happened to me when I was sixteen years old. Sex was pretty straightforward, right? You get a boner and you just go for it. "I think not," says the enlightened female.

After whatever resulting devastation passed, mechanical mind that I am, I was struck by the subsequent idea that there is a way *to be good at sex*, as if sex itself were an art that one could master like any other, such as playing guitar or mastering your golf swing. I read books like *She Comes First* by Kerner, *Urban Tantra*, and Indian classics like the Kamasutra. I spent a few years experimenting with partners and eventually, with a lot of patience, I improved. If nobody ever had the nerve to tell you the same thing, or you were so traumatized by the event that you decided to never be truly vulnerable again, you probably spent a few years drifting through sexual encounter after encounter, each one more disappointing than the last, until you arrived at one of two options, both of which represent extreme ends of the same spectrum. Either you looked towards religion for your answers in regards to sex, or you fell into rampant hedonism. We've all seen the extreme of both forms.

On one end of the spectrum, you have the hedonist who is always trying to get laid. Quantity over quality is the mantra. Settled firmly in the ego, these people will game just about anything that moves. It's not pretty. I've met many people like this in my travels. Usually they're younger, though I've met quite a few randy gray-beards who still see the entire universe through the narrow lens of carnality. Men like this see women only as instruments of pleasure. For them, nothing exists beneath the skin and certainly nothing between the ears. Chances are, if you're a woman reading this book, you've met a few of these borderline sociopaths. As it happens, I myself have met quite a few conquistadors of the fairer gender.

In the opposite direction, you have the religious fanatics who subscribe to a very limited and narrow understanding of what sex is and *should* be while viewing anything outside of the boundaries as sinful, heretical, dirty, baseless, and depraved. We typically see this in the form of Buddhist monks who aren't allowed to associate with women, Christian priests and nuns sworn to celibacy, or maybe your neighbor Bob who swears by the beard of God that he's never once masturbated. *Never.* In case you were wondering, he's full of shit.

People like this, should they have children, tend to shelter their offspring beneath a shroud of illusion before the now-grown adults wander into the world, only to be shattered upon the rocky shores of reality. In despair, they too turn to the very same extremism that gave them birth.

For those who live in a culture of abstinence, the reality has been dark throughout history. There's no shortage of religious leaders worldwide that have admitted to sex crimes against children in the past few decades alone. Many of these religious institutions go back thousands of years. It's hard to imagine the actual profundity of damage that has been caused by these religious zealots, who "too pure for sex," had to instead exercise their "baser" desires behind closed doors upon the helpless and impressionable.

Such a culture of extremes undoubtedly creates a collective neurosis in which nobody truly knows where to go. It helps little to find the middle path when you're assailed on both sides by shit. At the root, the collective neurosis that humans share around the subject of sex makes little sense when we really think about it. We're the only animal on the planet that loses hours of sleep over this. Other animals feel the urge, and they do it. There's no problem. It's only because humans have separated all of existence into dichotomies that we begin to see sex as a problem. Reproduction itself is what allows the animal kingdom to exist. Down to the smallest cell, there has always existed some way to divide and transmit what ends up being the replication of DNA and, therefore, the organism itself.

I won't be telling you any extreme version of sex. I won't be telling you, for example, that *sex* and *love* are one and the same. Though it surely can be expression of this emotion towards another human being, the average person will have too many casual rendezvous encounters to make such a point valid. I also won't be telling you that sex is just a frivolous play-thing, indistinguishable from any cheap toy that you can buy from the store. Human beings are not inanimate objects to be used for egotistical impulses and then subsequently discarded. We have feelings. You're rubbing sticks of fucking dynamite together every time you hop into bed with someone under false pretenses.

For the above reasons, I do not support the shallow Tinder culture that seems to permeate every part of dating within the younger generations (mine included), nor do I support the idiotic notion of "purity" that is so prevalent within zealous religious communities. Both make me sick, and both miss the mark. To socially enforce either will invariably lead to damage to the human beings who participate in the social narrative.

Sex is many things at once depending on how you view it. Biologically, it serves as a means for propagating our species. As we'll see, throughout our history as a species, sex was also a social transaction, a kind of glue which helped keep the tribe itself intact.

In relationships, however, sex is much more complicated. It can be the centerpiece of a loving relationship between two or more people; a casual, though not meaningless source of connection; and for the spiritually inclined, sex is the masculine and feminine energies yearning to be one. We'll see later that, with a little bit of consciousness applied, sex can be and *is* a literal act of worship in many traditions around the world. For now, let's talk about you and I. You and I are human. The average human being will have thousands of non-reproductive sexual encounters throughout their lives. Throughout the day, you and I will think, imagine, visualize, and fantasize about sex in some way, shape, or form for almost half of every minute that we spend breathing.

The fact that sex pervades every form of our advertising isn't a coincidence. We're bombarded by sexual memes every day, and the most hilarious jokes are often the most vulgar. Failing to see that humans are a hyper-sexual species is failing to look the ape staring back through the mirror. In any modern society, depending on the story being told about sex, it becomes clear that at least ninety percent of human energy is either running towards or running *away* from sex

If you're like me, having grown up in a Western paradigm, the story we are often told about sex and the relationships that lead to it is one that has over five thousand years of history by conservative estimates, backed by almost every organized religion from Christianity and Islam to Buddhism and Hinduism. It's a story of sanctity, of white dresses, flying doves, and church bells where two people give themselves completely to one another for life while renouncing the advances of all others. It's the story of monogamy.

Till Death Do us Part: Monogamy and Society

The Spanish word esposas means both "wives" and "handcuffs." In English, some men ruefully joke about the ball and chain. There's a good reason marriage is often depicted and mourned as the beginning of the end of a man's sexual life. And women fare no better. Who wants to share her life with a man who feels trapped and diminished by his love for her, whose honor marks the limits of his freedom. Who wants to spend her life apologizing for being just "one woman?"

-Christopher Ryan, Sex at Dawn

Word to the wise: I'm not a fan of most weddings. And unless you're a close friend, I'd honestly rather not come to yours. Statistics show that you and your spouse will be disillusioned with one another and emotionally destitute after only a few years. As of 2020, fifty percent of marriages will end in divorce. For the people that "just have no quit in them," whether through misguided religious views or through social reinforcement, the reality is often a loveless, sexless, and painful state of affairs; one that becomes a daily grind until one of you dies. Meanwhile, these toxic couples will often parade around for decades, presenting their relationship to the public as if it's "just perfect." "What are *you* doing wrong?" they will often say.

At this point, from what I've seen, I'm convinced that less than ten percent of the relationships that exist in society are genuinely based in sustained romance. The rest are mere caricatures of what they used to be. Far from criticizing the system itself, the failures are pointed back towards the human beings. "Surely," says the system of culturally enforced monogamy, "there must be something wrong with *you*." The failures are doomed to be rationalized later by well-intentioned relationship therapists: "Maybe he's just not ready for a relationship. He has commitment issues. He's scarred from his past. He has an inflated ego. There's an endless litany of rationalization for why men just can't cut it in a monogamous relationship. For women, the answer is usually a lot less polite. Women are usually just described as "fucking crazy."

Call me misinformed, but if almost everyone I know is playing a game marked by futile struggle when fifty percent of marriages will end with feelings of betrayal and disappointment, when there is an ongoing war beneath the roof of many a suburban home, when affairs seem to have become the rule rather than the exception, when the process of divorce is a *twenty-eight-billion dollar industry* that is growing even as I write these words, and when the very nature of the game has been shown to erode the emotional wellbeing of the people who play it, someone needs to go out on a limb and say it: *fuck that game.* It doesn't mean throwing the baby out with the bathwater, but considering the social nature of Homo sapiens, how we orient our relationships is in the same hand, how we orient our society. If the average human being is trapped within a toxic relationship, that person will take that toxicity into their everyday lives, and this is important.

It's exactly for the above reasons that I probably won't be at your wedding. Knowing the pain that will be caused to you; the feelings of shame, guilt and despair you'll endure as you try and salvage the romance that no longer exists; that you'll eventually become callused, dry and desolate, and maybe even cause others to become the same, it's simply out of the question. I feel like I'm participating in socially-enforced and ritualized *crime* every time I sit and awkwardly fidget in a crowd while two people say, *"I do."*

In case I didn't cover it in the last chapter, I'll say it now: you are *not* a solitary creature. Everything you do and say has consequences. It's as if you are a node, living within a vastly complex network, connecting you to all others. This is even more the case since social media became a reality, effectively placing mass advertisement in the palm of every modern human. Everything you do will affect the lives of others. So if you exist in a toxic state, how can you possibly affect others in a positive way? A more enlightened discussion of how we orient our relationships in society need to begin, and it needs to start with a firm biological basis of who we are as a species, not what culture insists we *should* be.

Despite many millennia of the failed social experiment, we are still told theory upon theory about how monogamy is completely natural in human beings, that it is in fact our instinct to bond in pairs. At its root, this is highly unlikely: among all mammals, only nine percent are strictly monogamous, and among primates, only twenty-nine percent exist in eternal pair bonds. Of the apes that do pair off, such as gibbons, the couple live by themselves forming nuclear families. It's a very rare occurrence that these groups come into contact with others.

Among social apes, there isn't a single species that exists in strictly monogamous relationships. Unless human evolution somehow took a one hundred and eighty degree turn, neither are we. The monogamy found in society is not a natural behavior, but something that is *taught* by culture. Virtually, every aspect of Western society falls into the monogamy trap.

If you've ever watched a Disney movie, you've no doubt run into the same narrative over and over. Whether it be Belle, Cinderella, or Ariel, each of these damsels are looking for their knight in shining armor. The knight himself is usually a wandering soul that just can't seem to find meaning in life. By finding *his girl*, the male protagonist presumably finds his purpose in life. Monogamy is often a central message in many of these movies. It's Rapunzel and Flint Rider; Belle and the Beast; Cinderella and Prince Charming. It doesn't stop with Disney either. Ever seen *The Notebook*, *The OC*, or *50 First Dates*? The reality is that if you live in Western society, you are bombarded with memes from birth that you are always looking for *that* person who is your missing piece, your *better half*, as the saying goes. Though rarely do we see the after-story of any of these narratives, and there's a reason for this. As passionate as the love affair may have been in the beginning, many a hot flame is destined to burn low.

As a culture, we are failing to look at the evidence against such a ridiculous notion. If you truly believe that monogamy is *the way*, you are failing to see the ape in the mirror, and you'll have hell to pay for your failure.

Seeing the Past Through the Present: Human Anatomy and Sex

"Every creature's body tells a detailed story about the environment in which its ancestors evolved. Its fur, fat, and feathers suggest the temperatures of ancient environments. Its teeth and digestive systems contain information about primordial diet. Its eyes, legs, and feet show how its ancestors got around. The relative sizes of males and females and the particulars of their genitalia say a lot about reproduction."

-Christopher Ryan

Show me a body, and I'll show you what the body is designed to do. Show me a cheetah, I'll show you a runner; show me an orca, I'll show you a swimmer; show me a crocodile, and we'll be looking at a cold-blooded killing machine. A sloth is made to stay out of harm's way, and an elephant is designed to uproot trees looking for food. As far as evolution is concerned, function follows form, and form feeds back into that function.

If you see a species surviving generation after generation in any environment, the only reason is because natural selection designed it to do so. What is the function, then, of a human body?

In the last chapter, we discussed the human brain and how it applies to our sociality. Now let's look at our bodies.

Taxonomically, humans are members of the great apes. The great apes include Gibbons, Orangutans, Gorillas, Chimpanzees, Bonobos, and us. A common ancestor between all of us lived twenty million years ago, the orangutan split off about fifteen million years ago, the gorilla eight million, leaving us with our closest cousins, the bonobos and chimpanzees who we humans split from around five million years ago.

What We Learn From our Closest Cousins

Humans, chimps, and bonobos bear striking resemblances if you cut beneath the skin. From the outside, it's very obvious that we are difference creatures, yet if you were to dissect a bonobo, a chimp, and a human and lay the opened bodies beside one another, you would have a very hard time telling one from the other. For anybody who doubts evolution, they should consider the likelihood of such an arrangement in *three separate* species. Murphy's Law implicated that you have a better chance of winning the lottery on three separate occasions in the same lifetime.

A mere cursory glance at the anatomy and behaviors of human beings immediately draws interesting questions in light of the theory of "natural" human monogamy. In human males, for example, you see the largest genitalia of any of the social apes, packed with enough sperm to father thousands of offspring during a lifetime. If the human male could but find the time and energy, each of us men could populate continents and countries.

In fact, many a rockstar and pro athlete have done exactly this (suffice it to say with not one, but many willing female volunteers). From an evolutionary standpoint, testis size in males draws a direct correlation with the amount of copulation the species is designed for. Whether we're talking about butterflies, reptiles, fish, or humans - a large testicle size in males is complimented by a population of receptive (otherwise known as horny) females, while smaller testis denote a species where females are reserved and stingy, always waiting for Mr. Right.

To add to this, the human male is also endowed with a scrotum, which acts as a temporary storage center for "ready to fire" sperm. For such anatomy to be present within a "naturally monogamous" species is the equivalent of finding a ready to go mini-bar in the house of someone who has never touched alcohol. Why have this in your house short of expecting a party to break out several times a week? The fact that Homo sapien's anatomy comes complete with a ready to fire sperm bank lends more to our rampant sexuality. None of this, however, flies in the face of contemporary ideas about sexuality as it pertains to men. After all, haven't men always been the shameless sodomizing half of the sexual dynamic within our species? Where it gets interesting is when you take a look at how a human female is built.

From a human female standpoint, the idea of the "coy" female holding herself in reserve turns out to be a caricature of what a human female actually is. Rather than being a natural behavior, women are taught by their society to be reserved in their sexuality. We have five thousand years of slut-shaming and notions of female "purity" to thank for this; not to mention state-sponsored ideas of chastity and the consequential murder of adulteress women who dared to live out their sexual desires.

Even today, women are brutally murdered in various large-scale societies throughout the Middle East, Africa, and parts of the South Pacific - stoned to death, hung by the gallows, burned alive, or simply shot like the dogs they are perceived to be by the people around them.

Cultural taboos cast aside, what we find beneath the hood of female anatomy tells a completely different story, effectively blowing the idea of female chastity out of the water.

The Ill-Fated Life of a Sperm

If you're a human sperm (as everyone reading this book once was), *you*, my friend, are a survivor of what was ultimately a suicide mission. During sex, the typical human male ejaculation will expel two to five milliliters of semen into the vagina, and within each mL are around one hundred million sperm. That means that every unprotected sex session ends with half a *billion* sperm being launched deep into the female reproductive system.

With such numbers to your advantage, pregnancy should be a sure thing, right? Wrong. The journey from cervix to egg is no easy affair. Frankly, your average person has better odds of climbing El Cap without a rope. Upon ejaculation, more than half of sperm die on impact. For those that survive, they must navigate what would be every soldier's nightmare - an acidic environment filled with leucocytes and antibodies, both of which roam around looking to destroy the invaders. As if the sperm don't have enough to worry about, they must then swim through the reproductive tract, which comes complete with many narrowing tubes of rapidly flowing fluids. Picture a school of salmon flowing upstream towards reproduction grounds, only replace the water with acid, *then* imagine a bunch of assholes throwing harpoons into the water just for fun, and you can begin to imagine the epic journey a sperm must make in order to reach the egg. In such an environment, it's a miracle a women can get pregnant at all. Indeed, if men didn't have such a high sperm count, our species would be extinct after a few generations.

The fact that a woman's reproductive tract is equipped with biological mechanisms to weed out competing sperm is a sign that humans are one of the many species that participate in what is called "sperm" competition, and this goes right into correlation with the male capacity for ejaculation. It makes little sense for evolution to endow men with such vast reserves of sperm count if it isn't placing a bet that at least one will survive the harrowing journey through a woman's reproductive system. In the same line, it makes little sense for a woman to be biologically endowed with such an effective sperm sorting system if she's not expecting many donations from many participants.

Aside from the female anatomy, human females also exhibit a behavior called female copulatory vocalization. In layman's terms, women make more noise in bed (round of applause for the screamers.). Add to this that women have a capacity for multiple orgasms within the same sex session while men are quick to reach orgasm, and you begin to theorize that the human female that is not only non-monogamous, but the exact opposite in sexual behavior. More on this later.

Body dimorphism, the average comparative size, between men and women is relatively small. The average man is only about fifteen percent larger than the average female, indicating that our species is more geared towards cooperation between genders rather than domination. Your average male gorilla will be twice the size of his female counterparts. Only the biggest and baddest gorilla will beat out other gorillas in order to gain sexual access to *all of the females*, which constitute a harem. The fact that your average man is relatively the same size as your average woman indicates that we have existed in cooperation, not domination. Though polygamy exists within human societies, it tends to be a fringe practice and one that is unsustainable in the long run. It turns out that men eventually get pissed off when they're not getting laid. It also goes without saying that any woman living within a harem is probably bored out of her sexually-repressed mind.

Such anatomy present within human beings alone should dismantle the idea that humans are naturally monogamous creatures. In the same vein, it should render obsolete ideas of purity and chastity championed by religious zealots who know nothing about the human body.

Though monogamy is largely the practice found throughout the world, this isn't the case with most hunter-gatherer tribes. Foraging tribes tend to be fiercely egalitarian, and this extends to all resources, including sexual partners.

Casual Sex: Getting Down and "Dirty" Around the World

From across anthropological literature, we find time and time again that pre-agrarian tribes from the Ache in Bolivia, the

Fuegians of Chile, the Kalahari Desert hunters in Namibia, the Canela of Brazil, and the Inuit of Northern Canada, casual sex practices occur at a frequent rate.

Obviously, there's a knee-jerk reaction to such a statement. The vast majority of us are more likely to characterize such tribal practices as dirty and barbarous. As we'll see, however, many casual sex practices have occurred throughout modern societies through elaborate rituals such as Saturnalia in Ancient Rome and Carnaval in Brazil. Why would this be? For a creature that is naturally monogamous, why would polyamorous behavior be recognized across the globe in such elaborate, culturally-sponsored rituals?

The Way of Nature

In nature, that which is unexpressed will eventually have to express itself. A fault line will eventually split causing an earthquake, a volcano will eventually blow its top, people who hold things in will eventually explode in emotional outrage, and human sexuality eventually always bubbles through the cracks of our culturally-enforced purity.

Let's ponder this question: what healthy roles could casual sex possibly play within a community, as well as within the human body? Knowing what we've covered with male capacity for sperm storage, a woman's ability to sort and weed out competing sperm in her system, and the social nature of Homo sapiens, how does it all apply?

Your average hunter-gatherer tribe will be characterized by multiple ongoing sexual relationships. You'll see the men copulating quite often with multiple women, while the average female such as that found in the Canela, the Ache, or Piraha will have had regular and ongoing sex with multiple men in her tribe through her ovulatory cycle. Accounts from missionaries, explorers, and ship captains alike are riddled with event after event of what is often called rampant and "sinful" behavior. Whether we're talking about the Tahitian tribes of Polynesia, the Fuegians of Chile, or the Inuit, the accounts are usually the same - a near scandalous sexual curiosity from tribal women towards outsiders and an almost routine practice of open sexuality that sometimes even ended in full-blown orgies for the explorers to witness or participate in. *A boa-vida.*

Because men are made with such vast quantities of reserve sperm, having regular sexual ejaculations throughout the cycle, there will be less subsequent readings of chromosomal damage within sperm. Regular sexual activity, then, will actually increase the ratio of healthy sperm to semen, thus *increasing* the sperm count of a man through heightened sexual behavior. Use it lose it, brother.

In women, such behavior means in the end that only the best sperm can win. A women's' reproductive defenses, though scary as they may seem to incoming sperm, are, in effect, a brilliant voting system, ensuring that infertility and genetic mutations will not be passed on to the next generation. In hunter-gatherer sexual behavior, only the strongest sperm can win, thereby helping to keep the gene pool clean. In addition, a woman's' ability to experience multiple orgasms allows us to better understand and interesting phenomenon, one that is often written off as a fetish in modern society.

The Insatiable Female

Within a society where women are shamed for having liberal sex lives, there's perhaps nothing worse than having a go with multiple people at the same time. After a quick search online, you'll find that one of the leading streamed genres on porn websites are, wait for it: the "gang-bang." Videos depicting multiple men with one woman effectively outnumber the opposite scenario (multiple women on one man) fifty to one. Let that sink in for a moment. If you're to believe the standard narrative, that men are naturally more sexual than their coy and reluctant female counter parts, why do men and women around the world on average invest more time viewing the very thing that tips this narrative upside down?

Multiple men on one woman is one of the most popular searches on porn networks throughout nearly every single culture among men and women alike, while multiple women on one man doesn't even come close. In light of the female anatomy, it makes sense, especially when we compare capacity for orgasm. And it makes even more sense given that peculiar female behavior we discussed earlier.

Why is it that women vocalize more during sex than men do? Such a behavior on the African savannah is risky to say the least, rendering the couple vulnerable to attack from predators and even other human beings. However, in light of the close-knit groups that women enjoyed being a part of, vocalization during sex suddenly makes sense. Indeed, among tribes such as Piraha of Brazil, the Tahitian tribes of the South Pacific, and desert hunters of the Kalahari, group sex occurs at incredibly frequent rates.

A woman's' capacity for orgasm, the sorting system she's endowed with for sperm competition, not to mention the almost universal human fascination with community sex, paints a picture of a creature much more erotic than we're led to believe. If we're to take a glance at our closest ape cousins, this is right on track. Among bonobos and chimps, we see a shameless and frequent amount of copulation, often provoked by the females themselves. Female chimps and bonobos alike often will mate with every male they can find. Jane Goodall, who has spent her life observing the apes, even reported seeing one particularly insatiable female mate fifty times in the same day.

If we're to lend an ear to our ape cousins, and evolution tells us that there is every reason that we should, we begin to see a human female that is not only sexually erotic, but in reality, *insatiable* compared to her male counterparts. The gang-bang, then, or "orgy" as it's often called, turns out to have been a normal practice throughout our history. It's only in the last few millennia that we've fetishized and scandalized the idea.

Now Let's Look at the Other Side of the Coin

If you've been in a monogamous relationship for more than a few years, the statistics indicate that you're probably not having much sex with one another. This is even more true if you're married. From a point of view of health and wellness, let's look at the potential health consequences of so little sex in a species that seems to be designed for frequent sexual encounters.

In men, infertility has been steadily climbing for many hundreds of years. In a monogamous relationship, the woman's' "voting mechanism" is rendered ineffectual. Having sex with only one man, she is, in turn, playing the lottery as to whether she'll be able to have children. Today, one in twenty men experience such a low sperm count that they have a hard time impregnating their partners. For those that eventually do get the job done despite their subpar fertility, the result can very well be a higher instance of children with low infertility, not to mention an incredible array of conditions associated with genetic mutations.

Monogamy also fails completely in two important roles – that of domestic affairs and the raising of children. Have you ever been to an orphanage? Has it ever struck anybody as ludicrous that orphanages could exist in the first place? Think about it for a second: you love your children so much, and you're aware that if you weren't there for them, they probably wouldn't stand a chance. Yet right this second, there are many children living in a foster care system because nobody wants to take care of them. Let that sink in. If you're a child in modern society, you are essentially playing the lottery.

You could be born into a dysfunctional household, one or both of your parents could die, leaving you to the foster-care system in certain countries, or on the street in others. Let's assume the best case scenario and place you in a house with two parents. Even then, the chance that you'll be subjected to domestic violence and perhaps even outright abuse is rather high. One out of three women in the United States have experienced domestic violence in the forms of slapping, shoving, and even beatings.

Rates of child abuse aren't much better. In 2019, there were over six hundred thousand reports of child abuse across the nation.

As with all statistics, it goes without saying that the reality probably reflects a much higher rate. These are just the cases that were *reported*. The fact that each monogamous household acts as a nuclear unit means that a culture of "mind your own house" becomes a reality. Unless they are particularly insensitive to societal cues, people will not invade the sanctity of another person's home even if it's evident that problems exist within the house's walls. Beneath the roof of many a suburban home, there is oftentimes an outright state of warfare going on. It's specifically because there is often no intervention from other parties, that the conflict between couples continues, and this is an important point.

The rates of abuse that take place in large scale society would never be permitted within a group where survival depends on the functioning of each individual towards the group cause. Abusive behavior would be checked by other members of the group. By sharing intimate relations with multiple people throughout the tribe, every member would be more or less aware of growing problems between certain members. The problems could then be remediated among the tribe before it turned into full-scale conflict, such is often the case in large-scale, nuclear-unit society. Along these lines we can then understand the role casual sex plays in hunter-gatherer groups.

It's a Networking System

Socially, casual sex throughout tribes provides the social glue that keeps the tribe cohesive. This isn't to say that anyone is drawing up a social contract for a sexual quota. No, but because sex is an intense form of social interaction, it makes sense that a social species such as Homo sapiens would partake in it quite frequently.

It's been shown that the expression of oxytocin, the same neurotransmitter responsible for pro-social feelings such as trust, is up-regulated directly after orgasm. Far from being a mere reproductive ritual, we can then understand that sex becomes a social transaction, often between many people at the same time. By partaking in sex, the higher levels of oxytocin mean that members of the tribe trust one another more. You're more likely to spill your secrets to someone you trust, thus setting the stage for a more empathetic atmosphere where problems can come to light and be dealt with. Is it perfect? Hell no. No system devised between human beings can be. We're far too complicated.

Partial paternity in the tribes means that children are much more likely to receive attention from the adult males of the tribe, while a woman can always expect the support of the men around her.

So in reality, the idea that women "don't want sex" turns out to be an excuse for *how* we're pursuing and having sex in the societies we live in. Sorry to break the news to you, brother, but the research is in: your girl is hornier than you are. You're just not the one getting the engine running. This begs the question: why is it true that women tend to not want sex within modern society? If hunter-gatherer life is characterized by rampant exploration of sex, what are we doing that's killing the vibe?

What Does All of this Mean for Monogamy?

In the preceding pages, I've used anatomy and physiology along with anthropological data to dispute the idea that monogamy is the natural way of human beings. This isn't to say that I disagree with it in practice. I wrote in the introduction that to be a primal human being includes doing what *you* feel is natural. Do you want a monogamous relationship? Then, by all means, have one. Just be ready to do the work that will be required. This is also not to say that polyamory is a cakewalk either. I've been polyamorous for three years. Let me tell you – you're constantly putting out fires, especially if you have multiple ongoing relationships at once. Relationships, whether multi-faceted or pair-bonded, are a difficult affair. This is life. Whichever way you choose, just know you are choosing a struggle.

For now I want to make it clear that there is nothing wrong with your way of dating and pursuing sex, as long as you aren't actively hurting other people in the process. Most importantly, *you* need to choose the lifestyle, not your society. The only thing that I will actively attack is any way of being that is *culturally enforced*, and that's exactly what we'll be talking about next.

Monogamy as a Culture

And what about marriage? To circle back to the original conversation, I do not disagree with marriage in practice. I frown upon what it currently represents in the form of enforced monogamy. You can hardly call marriage a monogamous practice, nor can any religion claim it as an original concept, though many try. Throughout human history and even in modern times, marriage has simply been a means of orienting relationships within society.

Marriage Characterized by Large-Scale Society

Socially enforced monogamy has a relatively short history in regards to human beings. Only ten thousand years of our history has been spent in monogamous societies, and yet, in a way, monogamy *is* the history of society. The pay-off for this, of course, is that by establishing these nuclear family units, each family unit then competes against others. By "keeping up with the Joneses," the resulting competition between each household spurs the growth of the economy, which then allows the society itself to grow.

Though humans share close ties with chimpanzees and bonobos, both of which are hyper-sexual as species, we form many of our societies as if we were gibbons, who live mainly with pair-bonding, forming nuclear family units that rarely tolerate the presence of other pair-bonds. In essence, we've taken a hyper-social, hyper-sexual body and sequestered it upon separated monogamous islands. How did such a thing happen in the first place, and why?

When we look at agriculture, we see many immediate changes in the behavior of human beings that apply to this subject. The group becomes sedentary, the group population increases, and the group obtains a surplus of resources. The three of these, when combined, set the stage for the accumulation of resources with *certain* individuals.

To hoard a tool or to take more food than your fair share, for example, in a hunter-gatherer society would constitute a threat to the entire group. Such behavior would be punished swiftly and contemptuously. Often the punishment would be death depending on the severity of the crime. This isn't the case with modern societies. In fact, the opposite phenomenon, accumulating wealth, is the very foundational stone by which society can exist. We call it personal property and without it, the drive to continue building society simply doesn't exist.

Because a surplus of resources means that property accumulates, that property becomes power. Those who have the most resources have the most power. From the roots of egalitarianism, you begin to see the seeds of the hierarchy being planted. Naturally, if you have many resources, you would like to have someone to give them to when you're gone, such as your children. As a powerful man, you therefore have to know *who your children are.*

We take for granted nowadays that we can identify paternity through scientific means. This simply wasn't the case thousands of years ago. The only way for a man be sure who his sons were was to prevent his woman from having sex with other men. Society itself would fall apart if women were running wild. The term "loose woman" denotes a female that nobody can be sure about in regards to paternity. Could be her husband, could be the mailman, maybe even the handsome barista at the cafe got her knocked up. Nobody knows. For this reason, society tends to regard such women with suspicion.

Thus, in order for monogamy to work, we must demonize, scandalize, and in some cases even prosecute women who dare to allow their natural inclinations come to fruition. "Natural inclinations" will no doubt elicit heated responses from many a pure and sanctified woman of the traditional view. Suffice it to say that these women will most likely be those who have been immersed within some form of religious ideology. If you think that I'm calling you a slut, fair enough. I am. The meaning of the word itself carries a connotation of promiscuity. By taking offense at the word, however, you are in the same hand demonstrating and perpetuating the very problem *I'm* attacking.

It's not being "slutty" that is the problem. We've already demonstrated plenty of human behavior characterizing humans as such. It is the meaning we apply to the word itself, which is all dependent upon the society you grew up in. If you grew up in Dayton, Virginia, chances are you grew up old-order Christian and were fed tales of how a proper woman is "modest" and "chaste." If you grew up in Saudi Arabia, even looking at a man in a seemingly erotic manner could land you in a world of shit.

In both cultures, you were taught to be ashamed of any sexuality that boiled to the surface, while in the same hand being taught to hide your body for fear of being a temptress to your male counterparts. Meanwhile, upon the coast of Brazil, women are prancing about in G-string bikinis, while in many parts of France and Spain, nude beaches seem to be the rule rather than the exception. Suffice it to say that none of this behavior is considered lewd to the people who live in those societies, which brings me back to the original point.

To any women out there bristling at the thought of being characterized as "erotic," "sexual," or "naturally" promiscuous, you should consider that *you* are the one characterizing these things as negative, and *you* are the one characterizing the behavior I'm describing as lewd.

Anatomy doesn't lie, my love. Show me your body, and I'll show you what it's made to do. As demonstrated through the analysis, humans both male and female have bodies that are capable of copious amounts of sexuality for a reason. If you don't find a healthy way to exercise that sexuality (emphasis on healthy), eventually your body will break down altogether, period.

Your argument breaks down even more if you argue in defense of monogamy, which at its root simply can't sustain the sexual relationships for human beings to be healthy. Sure, you might love your husband, and he might love you. The two of you might even have a healthy sexual relationship. Congratulations. Statistically speaking, however, you are the exception to the rule. Regardless of your situation, don't lie to yourself and say that monogamy is *about* love and *about* romance. It never was and never has been.

Monogamy, at the root of the practice, is more about simplifying the process of economics. Because each husband and wife constitute a unit, we can then keep track of how many resources each household has, thereby making inferences upon which households contain the most value. If women run throughout society, copulating to their heart's content, the resulting children will be a question mark. Men don't know who to leave their resources to, and the value of each household becomes blurred. Societal polyamory, for this reason, tends to be much less likely to be "prosperous," at least in how we think of the word under the current paradigm of global economics.

If you think that marriage has always been about love, you'd scratch your head to consider traditions around the world that contrast the view. In Bushido culture, for example, a wife ran the household, leaving the man free to train for war and service to his liege lord. The Japanese understood that duty and sexual attraction were two different things, and after a time period, couples simply weren't attracted to one another. Men had many courtesans as a result, and women were known to stray quite often under the radar.

Other cultures weren't as accepting of the realities of sex and how it plays a role in their lives. In the same time period in England, people were being branded as adulterers while the Spanish Inquisition was serving its own brand of torture to the adulterous.

Being an upstanding citizen in such societies meant exhibiting "proper" behaviors. Women were expected to be chaste and pure in their dealings, while men were to be noble and gentlemanly. Meanwhile, under the cover of night, men were ducking into many a brothel to rid themselves of their impure and base desires. In London alone during that period, there were well over forty thousand prostitutes to service your proper and polite gentlemen. It's hard to imagine how women must have suffered during these same times, having no outlet for which to exercise the same sexual impulses.

As unhealthy as this culturally sponsored behavior was, it nonetheless provided the benefit that men could know who their resources were being passed down to. Though they provided the order of the household, and therefore society, women were often reduced to second-class citizens. By limiting female sexual autonomy in a culture, the dynamic between men and women becomes sharply unbalanced. When this happens, we set the stage for the nature of relationships, and even of sex itself, to change.

When Men Run Amok

Once upon a time, it happened. A particularly disgruntled woman of the village walked up the mountain where it was rumored that a wise man lived. Upon her arrival, she was bathed in rose water and escorted to the man's dwelling. The old man was deep in mediation when she arrived, but he smiled merrily when she entered through the door. Though he was said to have many years, the man sat comfortably upon the ground, seeming to exhibit a vitality of many years passed. The skin beneath the gray of his beard was taut and without wrinkles. The woman noticed all of these things.

"Come, my lady," he said, flashing a smile "How may I be of service to you?"

Without preamble, the woman launched into her tirade: "Society is not fair," she began hotly. "I take care of the house, the children, and all domestic affairs, all while my husband runs around all night looking for other women to bed. Indeed, the man is a swine. I have heard from multiple sources of his infidelity, yet if I so much as look at another man, he becomes enraged with jealousy and accusation. The other women of my village just shrug, submitting to the infidelity of their own husbands. A woman was accused of cheating last week and stoned to death, yet, if my sources hold true, the men of the village are regularly committing the same crime with no retribution. The village priests offer no help in the matter. Indeed, they are often the worst of all, stealthily ducking into every brothel in town. In the village, a man is celebrated for bedding many women, only for the women he beds to be degraded and shamed for *his* exploit. In this way, one man's success becomes the very source of scourge for many women."

Throughout the tirade, the old man waited in silence, patiently nodding at all the right moments. "Why is it okay," she asked, trembling "for a man to pursue many women, but not for women to do the same? Tell me, please."

The man sat in quiet thoughtfulness. Finally, with a nod at the dead bolt upon the door, he said, "A key that can pick many locks is a wonderful key to have in your pocket, wouldn't you agree? But a lock that can easily be picked will surely leave your house open to every bandit in the village."

And with that, the old man rose and removed his clothes, revealing a wiry, muscular strength beneath. With a smile, he said, "You've journeyed all this way. Shall we?"

The woman glared through narrow eyes. Moments passed. "Well, why not?" she said finally. "But only if I get to have another bath." And there you have it.

When I was growing up in Virginia, I heard many forms of this same joke. While it helped to justify the growing sexuality within me that was always near boiling point, I was also aware of the double standard that catered to my favor and the subtle problem it presented to the women I grew up around.

What must it have been like to grow up in a society where you are taught to go against your biological impulses? That your purity and your *honor* were worth more to you than the many fulfilling experiences that were available to you?

For the woman that went against the grain, sex was often a disappointing and sometimes even painful experience. After all, nobody was teaching young adults *how to have sex*, and *how to date*.

Instead, at the age of ten years old, most of us were herded into classrooms where we were told extremely conservative narratives about sex. For me, and those unlucky enough to go through it with me, the story went something like this: *Sex is a sin. It should only be between a husband and wife. Having sex before marriage will lead to despair and eventually into hell. Should you decide to have sex before marriage, you have only STDs, unwanted pregnancy, and many shattered dreams to look forward to. By the way, here's how to put a condom on a banana. Have a good summer, and see you next fall.*

The culture that I lived in tended to cater to the same narrative. Parents tended to reinforce the same idea while community leaders such as pastors, coaches, and family friends would say the same thing, even as they themselves were probably failing to uphold their own standard.

Here's the reality: in any abstinence-based family life class, the vast majority of the kids in that classroom will have sex before marriage. And yet, we gear our education towards the few who decide to choose abstinence. Think about it for even a moment, and you realize that it makes absolutely no sense to cater to the minority if it will leave your majority naked (no pun intended) and unprepared for the reality that they will surely face. The art of sex isn't an easy one to figure out. And without proper, state-sponsored guidance, most of us are shooting arrows into the dark.

Wham, Bam, "Well, thank ya, ma'am!"

Sex is really not as straightforward as it might seem. For men, it seems this way. "We get an erection, there's a vagina. We just plunge in, right?" Such is the thought process of many a young man in a society with no education on how to have sex. The reality is that most of us suck at sex. I don't mean that lightly. We're really bad at fucking. This is especially true of men. I'm willing to bet that many of the women reading this book arc laughing at such an admission from a male, even if it is under their breath; while many men would like to see me stoned. Fair enough.

As mentioned earlier, I was the fortunate recipient of this information when I was sixteen. The reality, however, is that most women won't tell men up front to their faces. Why? Because despite all of our bravado, the male ego is a particularly weak phenomenon. When it breaks, there is often hell to pay, especially if a woman is responsible for breaking it. This can hardly be overstated. A negative statement from a male friend can hurt, yes. The same statement, however, from a women, especially one that you might have feelings for? That shit can wreck you. So what's a woman to do then?

Rather than risk the headache and maybe even potential physical danger, many women will simply accept the subpar performances, or just simply move onto the next man hoping that he's at least somewhat better than the last.

Meanwhile, there's room somewhere full of men proclaiming victory over last night's exploit. I've endured thousands of these banty-cock dialogues in my life - whether it was in locker rooms, on the field, the sauna, or out in the water surfing. Funny thing, the same phenomenon takes place among women, and as it happens, life once granted me a unique opportunity to witness such behavior.

Tales from Sodom and Gomorrah: A California Party Prop

In 2017 while still in the navy, I was stationed in Coronado, California. Money wasn't an issue while in the military, so it could only have been curiosity that possessed me to put in a job application with Butlers in the Buff, a company that hires fit-looking men in order to cater to bachelorette parties. We all know what happens at bachelorette parties. All sugar-coating aside, I was a stripper; paid to be half-naked and to show a good time to the women who were paying me to do so.

Typical activities at any party could range from standing around shirtless, serving drinks at cocktail parties, to going literally buck-wild with the women who hired us. In one particularly rowdy affair, my partner for the night was guy who we'll call "Brad." Brad was a student at San Diego State University and also worked as a fitness trainer at the local Gold's Gym. These parties were a way for him to blow off steam while earning a bit of extra cash on the side.

The night started off innocently enough, but it didn't take long for things to heat up. Having spent ten minutes in the kitchen pouring wine for the two dozen or so women at the party, I suddenly heard screaming. Not exactly out of the ordinary at a bachelorette party, you might think, but it seemed a bit early for such behavior to start. I arrived to the pool, tray in hand, to find a naked Brad stretched out upon the pool deck with a smile the size of Texas on his face. One girl was giving him a blow job while the other women were lining up to do cocaine off of his abs and biceps.

Another night, I found myself in a hot tub with the bride-to-be, wearing nothing but my bow tie. She, who shall remain nameless, had a "hall pass," for the weekend, so there was no foul play. In any case, I suppose it's only natural for a lady to go wild before she settles down into a prison of domestic affairs.

Whether a party was a "by the book" or "loosened tie" affair, there was always common thread: women like to talk, and boy, do women like to talk about men, especially in regards to the bedroom. Whereas male locker room talk seems to stop with "Did you get laid?" the same can't be said for the locker room dialogue among women. It's all about the details: how was the date, is he good kisser, how was his oral game, cock size (though not as much as you'd think), how long he lasted, whether there was any connection, and in general whether there was anything out of the ordinary that occurred throughout the night.

Sad to say, but it was very rare that I stood by listening to stories of exquisite male lovers. It was quite the opposite, in fact. Most of the stories ranged from subpar experiences to absolute nightmares for any woman to be in. One particular girl, let's call her Beth, told one particularly haunting tale of a man who obviously wasn't very good at oral sex. "It was like he trying to erase my clitoris with his tongue," she said. "Eventually, I faked an orgasm and said I wasn't feeling well," she said with a shrug. After countless evenings and countless stories told, the picture I had painted of American men in bed was that of mindless apes without a lick of sense.

After my experiences at Butlers in the Buff, I spent the next two years cultivating the idea that we men were the problem - that nobody taught us how to pleasure women, so we just did whatever came naturally to us. Sex is relatively straightforward for a man. We get an erection, we fuck, and we get out. Average penile-vaginal intercourse only lasts on average seven to fifteen minutes, while it often takes a woman much longer than this to reach climax. Penetration also fails to stimulate the clitoris, and thus tends to fail in facilitating the female orgasm. Since little to no discussion was happening between men and women on the subject, it was assumed that the men talking the cheek in the locker rooms truly believed they were *good* at sex. The reality was that it was often a teeth-gritting experience for the woman that endured their company. Plenty of literature on the art of sex confirms this.

A survey published in 2015 in *Cosmo* revealed that while men reached climax ninety-five percent of the time, it was only fifty-seven percent of the time that a woman would achieve even one orgasm. Sixty-seven percent of women admitted to regularly faking orgasms, but it doesn't stop there. Of the sixty-seven percent of women who admit to having faked an orgasm, a third of the same percentage admit to having had to grit their teeth through genuinely painful sex. It goes without saying that these statistics only reflect those who *admitted the truth*. The realistic numbers are probably much worse, as is usually the case with surveys of such nature.

I continued to believe that men were the problem, until a few particular encounters with women demonstrated that the problem is much more complicated than I ever imagined.

What the Hell is a G-Spot?

One night in May of 2019 while on leave, I met a girl in one of the local bars of my hometown. Let's call her Maya. Maya was a communications major at the local James Madison University. We had drinks together, she told me of her childhood, and the evening ended back at her place. We lit a candle, put some Ziggy Alberts on the playlist, and spent the next hour or so doing what humans do, which for Maya ended with an explosive orgasm. As we lay down together afterwards, exhausted, she asked me what I did.

I asked her what she meant. "Nobody has ever done *that* during oral sex," she began. "Most guys skip it entirely." I rolled my eyes knowingly. By this point, I wasn't surprised to hear that many of my fellow males time and time again tend to skip oral (big mistake, gents.) Nonetheless I was still perplexed and asked her to be more specific about what *"that"* was. I could see that she couldn't explain in the slightest detail. So I elaborated briefly on the moments just before her orgasm.

Having just read Ian Kerner's *She Comes First*, I was readily armed with the anatomy of the female vulva. I told her that while I was down on her, as I noticed the tension developing in her thighs (that subtle shaking that starts when a women's climax starts to build), I kept my tongue on her clitoris, while using my fingers to press up against the G-spot, a branch of nerves the size of a quarter just inside the vagina. By doing this, you massage and stimulate the clitoral network from both sides, which can send a woman over the edge if the tension has built enough. I thought the explanation would be sufficient. "What the hell is a G-spot?" My eyes flew open, and I sat up. She had to be joking.

I had no idea what to say. A woman who didn't know what the G-spot was? The idea was ludicrous to me. Until this point, I had assumed that women were sexually enlightened creatures who knew exactly how to pleasure themselves and exactly what they wanted from men. The fact that I was giving an anatomy lesson to a woman about *her* body struck me as something purely out of left field.

And yet, after that evening, I became aware over and over again of the sobering fact: it's not just men who don't know what they're doing. Most women don't either, which makes sense. Unless you live in a particularly enlightened part of your country, nobody is teaching women how to express their sexuality, and definitely not how to *explore* their sexual potential. This was the first event that I realized how complicated the conversation between men and women actually is. The second took place during my first trip to Brazil.

"I'm Just not Feeling Good"

Word to any young gringos out there, if you're looking to explore sex, go to Brazil. If you can manage to keep your head out of your ass, you'll have no problems meeting women. As they say in Portuguese, *A brasileira adora o gringo.* Truer words were never spoken.

However, not everything is love and sex beneath the shade of the jungle trees. I learned this one night out in Itacare, a small surf town on the coast of Bahia. I'd gone down to Brazil to work for a volunteer organization that protected and replanted the mangrove forests in the region. A few fellow volunteers and I spent the night hopping around bars, letting loose. One of the volunteers had a friend visiting from Sao Paulo. Let's call her Juliana. Beautiful, blonde, curvy, eyes the color of glacial ice - the kind a guy can get lost in. Need I say more? We connected pretty quickly, and it wasn't long before we were walking back to my small house in the volunteer space.

When we got back to my house, we immediately started kissing and removing each other's clothes. Within moments, I could tell that something was wrong. She just wasn't showing enthusiasm that one would expect. My mind raced with every possible thought. *Do I stink? Is it my breath? The poke bowl? My God, why did I choose spicy salmon? Maybe she's sick? How often to people change their bed sheets?* After about two solid minutes of my internal monologue eating me alive, I pulled away. Holding her at arm's length, I asked her if she was all right. Suddenly, she seemed really nervous at the question.

Her answer surprised me. "I just don't feel good right now. I really like you, but I just think we're going too fast, and it doesn't feel right."

I was relieved to say the least. I told her that it was fine. "No stress. If you want we can just lay down and talk." She seemed shell-shocked at hearing this, as if she'd never heard it before in her life. Nonetheless, watching me put my clothes back on, she did the same and we laid down in my bed.

We lay there talking for the better part of an hour while the summer rain fell upon the tile roof above. She told of her life, past dating experiences, her job in Sao Paulo, how she'd love to move to Itacare and travel more. Despite the fact that we didn't have sex, it was one of favorite nights of that first trip to Brazil. There's something nice about lying down with somebody, trusting them, and knowing that they trust you in return. We fell asleep together.

The next morning, I woke up thinking nothing in particular of the night before until the following evening. We ducked out of a movie with friends, making some excuse that we were tired, and headed to my house. After the sex, Juliana admitted to me the truth of the night before. She told me that normally, under similar circumstances, she would have gone ahead and had sex with the guy she was with even if she wasn't feeling well. She told me that because I had "invested" my time in her and had left the party and the nightlife, that she had felt obligated towards me, and that she was afraid of disappointing me. This blew my mind. Prior to this experience, I had never before thought that such a thing was even possible.

If we understand sex at its core and we understand the attraction of the polarizing masculine and feminine energies, we understand *why* sex happens in the first place. Because these two are polar opposites of the same dichotomy, they are constantly striving towards one another. Sex is the mechanism by which the masculine and feminine can finally come home, briefly as it may be. This is why sex is so important between couples. It's only when the energies are connected that men and women tend to feel comfortable talking to one another about deeper aspects of the relationship. Sex is a gift to us in this regard. But to have sex when you don't feel right? Because you see it as an obligation? A *service* rendered because someone *invested in you?* What the fuck… it was too much for me to digest in one sitting.

What she told me that night traumatized me on many levels. On one level, I thought about my mother and sister, and the possibility that they'd ever had to go through the same ordeal that Juliana had to in her past. To go through the process of having sex with someone through obligation, or worse, because they were intimidated by the possible consequences of *not having sex.* Think about it: though the average male is only fifteen percent larger than the average female, this is still enough to be intimidating. Men are, on average, physically stronger not to mention more aggressive than the average girl.

Even worse, I thought of the women in my life that I had been with. Standing at six-foot-three and weighing in at two hundred pounds with my reddish-blonde hair and beard, I'm told that I can be a little intimidating upon first glance. Add to this the fact that I'm usually concentrating on an aggravating bit of philosophy or writing, and I have what you could call a resting frown. Altogether, the effect is probably something of a Scottish Highlander pondering out who to fight next. It's definitely not the most welcoming sight for first impressions. And though I've never had the slightest intention of harming or forcing a woman to have sex, the women who have known me perhaps didn't know that.

How many women have *I* intimidated in the past without meaning to? How many women slept with me simply to *follow through?* How many women are doing that exact thing this very moment, and what's worse, how many members of my gender would use this knowledge to their advantage?

It turns out that when we really get down to the root of societies that are heavy in masculine energy, this kind of dynamic can be very common, as tends to be the case in Brazil, the United States, and across the Middle East. You end up with what is a machismo culture in which men will inevitably come to expect women to cater to their needs while rarely giving in return.

In such a culture, sex stops being about connection and depth and instead about service and, in some cases, a form of domination and degradation. To be fair, domination has its place in the bedroom. Many women like to be handled roughly and there are reasons for this. But not *all the time, gents.*

Because sex becomes a form of service to men, we can suddenly wrap our minds around all the brutal porn that is present and in growing popularity on porn websites. Hop on PornHub for even a moment, and you'll encounter videos that commonly feature names such as "Her Limit," "No Mercy," or for the particularly dark-souled aficionado, "Destroyed."

And because we have a whole generation growing up on social media and the porn that comes with it, we'll have an entire generation whose sex education will be founded upon these particularly dark manifestations of carnality.

God help us.

Society is a Dance of Polarity

The same polar opposites that meet in the bedroom are also the same polarities that personify a society. Masculine energy is characterized by aggression, drive, and endurance. When you watch a skyscraper go up, a jet plane being built, or a football team breaking through the defense of another, you're looking at masculine energy in action. Masculine energy, by nature, is that of competition.

Feminine energy is marked by empathy and compassion. When we see a person caring for the defenseless, when we see two people in empathetic embrace, and when we see self-sacrifice for others, we are witnessing the expression of the feminine. Cooperation is the mark of the feminine.

The differences between any given society from another can be boiled down to how the masculine and feminine energies are corresponding to one another. In a society, for example, such as in Afghanistan where women have little voice, you can expect to find an increasingly aggressive society characterized by masculine energy. Indeed, due to the culture of honor still prevalent in much of Afghanistan, you could be killed simply for looking at another person in the wrong way. The same is true for hyper-masculine cultures such as the Scots-Irish of the eighteenth century, and the culture of honor that was and still is prevalent throughout the Appalachian Mountain chain.

Throughout all of these masculine cultures, sex is often a taboo, and even looking at another man's woman with interest could get you a walk to the chopping block, and homo-sexuality could very well be a life-or-death affair. As mentioned earlier, whether or not a child has a healthy home situation is a roll of the dice at best. Far from taking care of the orphans, masculine societies are often characterized by rationalizations of why the people are worse off than others, thus relinquishing anybody from responsibility. It pays to mention that in many masculine societies, the spiritual text spinning the narrative often marks "taking care of the widows and orphans," as a foundational stone. Why remind people in society to do this if it's not an inherent problem? Whether or not the society fails to keep in line with the rule is anyone's guess.

Meanwhile, you have societies around the world marked by feminine energy, such as the Minangkabau of Sumatra and the Mosou of Southern China. Here, women are the heads of the households, while the head of any family will be the grandmother. Inheritance of land goes from mother to daughter. Both of these societies tend to be about cooperation rather than the competition so implicit in masculine societies. Sexuality among the Mosou is defined by what are called "walking" marriages. When two lovers take a walk, whether heterosexual or homosexual, they are considered married for the duration. When the interest is no longer there, they can part ways with no strings attached. Resulting children from the walking marriages are raised within the households of the women, and paternal care is provided by her brothers who live with her. A man can decide to be there for his biological offspring, but his primary responsibility will be in taking care of his sisters' children, who are the result of *her* lovers. Quite the head spin, I know. In this way, however, childcare is always ensured, and many a woman never need to wander the streets looking for a way to take care of herself and her children.

Are We to Compete or Cooperate?

What shall the foundational stone of a society be? As mentioned earlier, depending on the nature of society, humans can orient themselves either like chimps or bonobos. Shall we be marked by competition existing in constantly shifting male coalitions, or shall we exist through cooperation to ensure the welfare of everyone involved? For me, I'd prefer a combination of the two. Growing up with three older siblings, I'm hyper-competitive by nature. I have an older brother named Cody. Whether it's a game of Madden, beer pong, chess, or throwing darts, Cody and I are looking to see who is better. Even when throwing a football between one another, the game inevitably becomes, "Who will drop the ball first?" We start throwing harder and harder until both of us work up a sweat. There's no problem with this.

Competition is perfectly natural and is the mark of many of our favorite pastimes throughout society. Through competition, people are often united on a massive scale, as anyone who has ever been to the World Cup or an NFL matchup can attest. My view, however, as it pertains to society is that competition should never be the foundational stone itself because then "who is better," becomes more important than "How healthy is everyone as a whole?"

Think of global economics, for example. We put so much of our time and energy into figuring out who on the global scale has the strongest economy. Thus the system that defines our current world is really just a game. In order to play the game, those that have the highest score will do just about anything to keep their place in the standings. Think of the United States, for example. A large portion of the economy is based on a medical system that requires people to be sick in order to function. We invest in medical insurance premiums which then require us to buy into habits which land us in the hospital. Cigarettes, hard alcohol, preservative-laden food, and a culture of overwork become the norm while the people who buy the products are robbed of their health. "But the economy is booming," they say. Such countries will do anything, poison their own people, even destroy the surrounding environment that sustains them if it means maintaining their rank.

On the other hand, however, I'm not convinced that a society marked purely by feminine cooperation is the ideal situation either. Such an orientation could potentially belittle the well-documented male need for competition. In the end, we need balance between the two energies.

The patriarchy as it's defined is any societal structure that is defined by masculine energy. You'll find no shortage of aficionados on the subject claiming that it is a man's rightful place to rule over women. It's easy to see why masculine energy would dominate when there is something worth fighting over. Masculine energy is partially marked by aggression and drive, so when it comes to dividing up resources, such as those that became a reality in post-agricultural communities, it makes sense that the more aggressive masculine energy would take over. The patriarchy is but the manifestation of masculine energy too far out of balance.

We have subscribed to the belief that men and women are so different, and the result has been a relationship orientation based more on separation rather than common ground. For this reason, books like *Men are from Mars, Women are from Venus* have become international best-sellers. Let's be clear. Men and women evolved together, and we evolved to help each other, not to exist in perpetual turmoil. It's only because we have subscribed to the belief that we are so different that we have become separated. Sex has become a mere expression of that separation. Instead of lovingly connecting with our partners, we have become more likely to dominate and degrade them.

Men and women exist to complement one another. We exist in a dance, like yin and yang. The problem is that we've forgotten how to dance. It's for this reason, perhaps, that certain traditions around the world turned sex into a literal act of worship in order to always keep this knowledge front and center.

A Brief Summary of Tantra

All Life is Energy

When Albert Einstein told us that E=mc2, what he was essentially saying is that all existence is energy.

The entire periodic table of elements is the same energy, only concentrated in different combination. The elements themselves give birth to every form of matter you know of. Whether you are talking about a speck of sand, a piece of wood, a star in space, or a human being, you are looking at different manifestations of the same energy.

To add a layer of spirituality upon the science, then, is to say that God is nothing more than the energy that allows matter to exist - From the stars in the night sky to the life on Earth looking up and spinning philosophy about it. Knowing that the same energy that exists within you is the same that animates all life – it's only a small step from there to see how you and I are connected to not only one another, but all other forms of life.

It's for this reason maybe that sex is often practiced as a literal act of worship among many human beings around the world.

Yoga and Tantra

Tantric sex has become more and more popular through mainstream media. There's no shortage of articles online about tantric positions that couples can try, couples breathing practices, and, of course, the legend of the "multi-orgasmic male." With a culture so obsessed with sex, it makes sense that we would take an ancient tradition of incredible profundity and apply it only to our shallow interests. Saying that tantra is about sex is much like saying that yoga is a just a physical workout. It can be, as many a Hatha yogi knows. By doing so, you are only fixating upon one branch of a deep and nourishing system of spiritual exploration.

Tantra means technology, and the goal of this technology is to connect with the divine in whatever form that divinity shows itself. Whether you are a devout Christian, Muslim, Hindu, or Pagan, you are trying to connect with some unknown force, and you are therefore using a method of tantra. Once you achieve connection with that force, you arrive at mysticism, and the connection becomes more important than the religion itself.

To put it metaphorically, religion is a boat. It can get you safely across the river, but once you are across, the boat is no longer needed. In fact, to drag its dead weight can become a source of misery to you. To practice tantra is to come to the realization that God dwells within you, in every human being, and in every speck of existence from the atomic to the cosmic.

Human beings hurt each other only because they fail to see that they are connected to one another. Suppose I was to give you a knife and then tell you to cut off one of your fingers. Would you do it? Short of the deranged and psychotic, I assume you wouldn't. Why?

You wouldn't cut off your finger because your finger is a *part* of you, and one that you depend on very often throughout your existence. The same is true of your environment and the life that inhabits this space with you. The problem is, we are under the illusion that we don't depend on the environment. In fact, because we believe nature is out to get us, we actively destroy nature. If you could but view all of existence in the same way you view your finger, would anyone have to tell you not to pollute the air we breathe and the water we drink? Would anyone have to tell you not to litter? Would it be necessary to have groups that protect and petition to *save* the environment? No. Furthermore, if you could view your partner with the same reverence you give to God, if you could sense the divinity within them, how much more connected could you be with them? How would it change the way you have sex with them?

Tantra and Sex

We all came from sex. It is the core of our existence. Somehow, instead of holding it as sacred, we have turned it into something dirty and shameful. Because we feel sex is shameful, we feel that shame within our bodies and minds every time we feel a desire bubble to the surface. We look at other people and we think,

"What would they think of me if they knew they dirty desires I have within my head?" Meanwhile, those same people are thinking the same thing. In such a state, we turn away from life instead of living it, demonizing the process of life more and more as we run.

Upon every human soul is draped a human body. That body is a means by which to feel the world through a sensual nature. Remember that the next time you have any feelings of genuine sensuality. That feeling is God acting through you. Once you realize this, you can once again be human and you can do what humans were made to do, only now in a healthy way.

The Eye Connection

Beyond the philosophical idea, I am not a teacher of tantra, and aside from one simple exercise, this will not become a guide book to practice.

They say you can see someone's soul through the corridors of their eyes. Maybe for this reason, eye contact seems to be becoming less and less frequent in today's world. Think about it: when is the last time you stared deeply into the eyes of another person? It's very unlikely that you have, and yet there's great power in doing so.

It goes without saying that you can do this with a friend, but for now, let's focus on couples. Sit down across from one another in a comfortable position. Place your right hand upon their chest, while letting them do the same. Place your left hand over the hand resting upon your chest while they also do the same. By doing this, you create an infinity loop of energy transaction. The touch upon so intimate a spot will initially create some fear, but eventually the brain will release oxytocin.

As you begin to gaze deeply into the eyes of your partner, begin to breathe together. Inhale slowly and deeply matching their rhythm, feeling their chest expand beneath your hand as they feel yours in return. With each breath cycle, the mind will begin to slow, and your awareness will grow. Do this exercise for two to three minutes and watch what happens.

Confronting Light of Day

Have you ever heard the "Allegory of the Cave" by Plato? It's a fascinating metaphor and one that applies deeply to the current human struggle with sexuality.

The allegory centers upon a family imprisoned within a cave. At the center of the cave is a fire, the light of which is cast outward upon the cave walls. As the light bounces of the stone it creates shadows upon the walls which fascinate the people observing the interplay of light. Eventually the family becomes so entranced by the interplay that they devote all their energy to maintaining the fire which has become their source of truth. The people don't understand that what they are seeing upon the walls are mere phantoms and shadows, unreflective in the least of the truth of the world.

Human beings are the only animal on the planet that have allowed our sexuality to become a problem. By lending an ear to religious institutions, we have allowed ourselves to become disconnected from our nature as human beings, and thus we have become disconnected from the life-process itself. We cannot continue like this.

Society is created collectively by men and women. Both of us are needed for this thing called life to work. Tantric philosophy and practice aside, men and women need to find connection once more. We can only do that once we accept our deeply ingrained sexual nature.

Only together can we walk out of the cave. And only together can we feel without shame the sun's warmth upon our naked skin.

Conclusion

The Journey Home

Perhaps the most intriguing part of being human is that in virtually every culture in the world, the myths and fables that hold the culture together are comprised of a single central narrative: The Hero's' Journey. Take any famous epic tale: Gilgamesh, Beowulf, Robin Hood, Luke Skywalker, Thor. These are all tales of human endeavor in which the protagonist is called to action, and through struggle and pain must gain a missing piece. They leave security and safety in order to pursue this goal. In the end they can return home to share the new gift of knowledge with their people.

All religions, by default, follow the same narrative. The central theme of the Judeo-Christian epic is how humanity has lost connection with God, and the sacrifice that is required to return home to the divine. The entire Bible is but a vast compilation of stories describing what happens when people succeed in their sacrificial offerings to God, as well as the horrors that follow when they don't. Buddhism holds that all life is suffering. The path out of suffering involves connecting with the truest depths of who you are. The Sutras describe the path to unlocking those depths.

In every tale, the hero must leave home. This is Abraham leaving his father's tent, Siddhartha leaving the palace, even Harry Potter leaving the Dursleys.

Agriculture took us away from our roots. With every loss along the road, we have also acquired new gifts. Knowledge, philosophy, technology, and new systems offer to connect us to the world-entire. This book has been about the journey that can bring us back home to our nourishing roots, and how we can even bring a few gifts back.

We have the road in front of us, the one that can take us back to our nature as human beings. Shall we take the walk...or not?

www.ingramcontent.com/pod-product-compliance
Lightning Source LLC
Chambersburg PA
CBHW050910260726
48660CB00001B/131